A GRAMMAR
OF THE
BENGALEE LANGUAGE.

A

GRAMMAR

OF THE

BENGALEE LANGUAGE.

BY

THE REV. W. CAREY, D. D.

GYAN

Published by

GYAN

Gyan Publishing House
5, Ansari Road
Daryaganj, New Delhi-110002
Phone: 011-47034999, 9811692060
E-mail: books@gyanbooks.com

Distribution Network
gyanbooks.com
India, USA, Canada, UK, Australia, France

ISBN: 978-81-212-7935-2 (PB)
First Published, 1801

2nd Impression 2023

Printed at: Gyan Press, Delhi.

A GRAMMAR OF THE BENGALEE LANGUAGE
Author: W. CAREY

A GRAMMAR

OF THE

BENGALEE LANGUAGE.

A

GRAMMAR

OF THE

BENGALEE LANGUAGE.

THE FIFTH EDITION.

BY

THE REV. W. CAREY, D. D.

Professor of the SUNGSKRITA *and* BENGALEE *Languages, in the* COLLEGE *of* FORT WILLIAM.

FROM THE SERAMPORE PRESS.

1843.

PREFACE

TO

THE THIRD EDITION.

BENGAL, as the seat of the British government in India, and the centre of a great part of the commerce of the East, must be viewed as a country of very great importance. Its soil is fertile, its population great, and the necessary intercourse subsisting between its inhabitants and those of other countries who visit its ports, is rapidly increasing. A knowledge of the language of this country must therefore be a very desirable object.

The pleasure which a person feels in being able to converse upon any subject with those who have occasion to visit him, is very great. Many of the natives of this country, who are conversant with Europeans, are men of great respectability, well informed upon a variety of subjects both commercial and literary, and able to mix in conversation with pleasure and advantage. Indeed, husbandmen, labourers, and people in the lowest stations, are often able to give that information on local affairs which every friend of science would be proud to obtain. The pleasure and advantage, therefore, of free conversation with all classes of people, will amply repay any person for the labour of acquiring the language.

An ability to transact business, and inspect all the minutiæ of mercantile concerns, without the intervention of an interpreter, must be an object of importance to every one engaged in such undertakings; and in the important concerns of administering justice, collecting the revenues, and preventing impositions and misunderstandings in all the common affairs of life, the disadvantages to which every one is subject who is ignorant of the language, not only plead in favour of the study thereof, but strongly mark the necessity of acquiring it.

A benevolent man feels much pleasure in making enquiries into, and relieving the distresses, of others. But in a foreign country he must be unable to do this, to his own satisfaction, so long as he is unacquainted with the current language of the country; for should he attempt to do it through the medium of servants, he would not only be liable to innumerable impositions, but his kind intentions must be frequently rendered abortive by the ignorance or inattention of those to whom the management thereof is committed.

The advantages of being able to communicate useful knowledge to the heathens, with whom we have a daily intercourse; to point out their mistakes; and to impress upon them sentiments of morality and religion, are confessedly very inportant. Indeed, the high gratification which must arise from an ability to contribute in any degree to the happiness of a body of people supposed to be equal to the whole population of Great Britain, can scarcely fail of recommending the more general study of the Bengalee, a language which is spoken from the Bay of Bengal in the south, to the mountains of Bootan in the north, and from the borders of Ramgur to Arakan.

It has been supposed by some, that a knowledge of the H*i*n-d*oo*sthanee language is sufficient for every purpose of business in any part of India. This idea is very far from correct; for though it be admitted, that persons may be found in every part of India who speak that language, yet H*i*nd*oo*sthanee is almost as much a foreign language, in all the countries of India, except those to the north-west of Bengal, which may be called Hind*oo*sthan proper, as the French is in the other countries of Europe. In all the courts of justice in Bengal, and most probably in every other part of India, the poor usually give their evidence in the dialect of that particular country, and seldom understand any other; which is also usually the case with the litigating parties.

In Bengal all bonds, leases, and other agreements, or instruments, are generally written in the current language; and the greater part of those persons with whom a European is concerned, especially in the collection of the revenue, and in commercial undertakings, speak no other : to this may be added, that, with a few exceptions, those who have a smattering of Hind*oo*sthanee, speak it too imperfectly to express their sentiments with precision.

The Bengalee may be considered as more nearly allied to the S*u*ngskr*ita* than any of the other languages of India ; for though it contains many words of Persian and Arabic origin, yet four fifths of the words in the language are pure S*u*ngskr*ita*. Words may be compounded with such facility, and to so great an extent in Bengalee, as to convey ideas with the utmost precision, a circumstance which adds much to its copiousness. On these, and many other accounts, it may be esteemed one of the most expressive and elegant languages of the East.

Since the first and second editions of this work were published, the writer has had an opportunity of studying this language with more attention, and of examining its structure more closely than he had done before. The result of his studies he has endeavoured to give in the following pages, which on account of the variations from the former editions, may be esteemed a new work.

W. CAREY.

Serampore, March, 1818.

A GRAMMAR, &c.

SECTION I.

Of Letters.

THERE are fifty letters (অক্ষর) in the Bengalee Alphabet, of which thirty-four are consonants (ব্যঞ্জন), and sixteen vowels (স্বর).

CONSONANTS.

ক	খ	গ	ঘ	ঙ
k*a**	kh*a*	g*a*	gh*a*	gnoo'*a*
চ	ছ	জ	ঝ	ঞ
ch*a*	chh*a*	j*a*	jh*a*	gnee'*a*
ট	ঠ	ড	ঢ	ণ
ṭ*a*	ṭh*a*	ḍ*a*	ḍh*a*	n*a*
ত	থ	দ	ধ	ন
t*a*	th*a*	d*a*	dh*a*	n*a*
প	ফ	ব	ভ	ম
p*a*	ph*a*	b*a*	bh*a*	m*a*
য	র	ল	ব	—
j*a*	ṛ*a*	l*a*	b*a*	—
শ	ষ	স	হ	ক্ষ
sh*a*	sh*a*	s*a*	h*a*	khy'*a*

---

* In repeating the alphabet, the short inherent vowel has the sound of aw, but is sounded much shorter when the letters are formed into words. *See remarks on the sounds of the letters.*

VOWELS.

অ	আ	ই	ঈ
a	a	*i**	ee
উ	ঊ	ঋ	ৠ
oo	oo	r*i*	ree
ঌ	ৡ	এ	ঐ
l*i*	lee	e	i
ও	ঔ	অং	অঃ
o	ow	ung	oh

1. The first five classes of letters are called বর্গীয়, (belonging to a class) from বর্গ, *a class*, and are respectively denominated ক-বর্গ, চ-বর্গ, ট-বর্গ, ত-বর্গ, and প-বর্গ, from the first letter of each class. The other nine letters are called অবর্গীয়, or miscellaneous.

2. The first and third letters of each class are unaspirated (অল্পপ্রাণ); the second and fourth are aspirated (মহাপ্রাণ), and the last of each class is a nasal (সানুনাসিক).

3. The vowels are short (হ্রস্ব), as অ, ই, উ, ঋ, ঌ; or long (দীর্ঘ), as আ, ঈ, ঊ, ৠ, ৡ.

4. They are also similar (সমান), as অ and আ, ই and ঈ, উ and ঊ, ঋ and ৠ, and ঌ and ৡ; or dissimilar (অসমান), as অ and ই, ই and উ, উ and ও, &c. viz. every vowel is similar to itself, and to its corresponding long or short vowel, and, consequently, dissimilar to all others.

5. য, র, ল, ব, and হ are the semi-vowels, and ঙ, ঞ, ণ, ন, and ম are the nasals.

---

* Italic letters must always be pronounced short in giving the sounds of Bengalee words.

6. The five classes are so arranged that every letter in the same class is pronounced with the same organ, *i. e.* the ক-বর্গ, are gutturals, the চ-বর্গ, palatines, the ট-বর্গ, linguals, the ত-বর্গ, dentals, and the প-বর্গ, labials. The other consonants and the vowels are classed with the বর্গীয় letters as follows:

কণ্ঠ্য, or Gutturals: অ আ এ হ্ ক খ গ ঘ ঙ.
তালব্য, or Palatines: ই ঈ চ ছ জ ঝ ঞ শ এ ঐ য.
মূর্দ্ধন্য,* or Linguals: ঋ ৠ ট ঠ ড ঢ ণ র ষ.
দন্ত্য, or Dentals: ঌ ৡ ত থ দ ধ ন ল স ব.
ওষ্ঠ্য, or Labials: উ ঊ প ফ ব ভ ম ব† ও ঔ.

On the Pronunciation (উচ্চারণ) *of the Letters.*

ক sounds exactly as the English k.

খ is the same letter aspirated. The sound will be best expressed by the junction of k and h in the English word bric*k*-*h*ouse.

গ is g hard as in gate.

ঘ. The same letter aspirated, like g-h in lo*g*-*h*ouse.

ঙ. This letter is seldom used in its simple state, but is commonly compounded with another letter, as ঙ্ক ngk*a*.

চ, ছ. The first of these letters is ch, as in *ch*urch; the other is sounded with an aspirate, as chh in mu*ch* *h*aste.

---

* This word properly signifies head letters; they have been generally called cerebrals.

† According to some, this letter is sometimes dental and sometimes labial; it is therefore inserted as belonging to both organs.

In the southern parts of Bengal both of them have a sound resembling that of s.

জ, ঝ. Are j and its corresponding aspirated letter; these are often, though improperly, pronounced like z and its aspirate. The proper sound is expressed by j in *j*ust, and ge-h in Coll*ege-h*all.

ঞ is very seldom used, unless compounded with another letter, as ঞ্জ nj*a*.

ট, ঠ. The English t and its corresponding aspirated letter. The aspirated letter must never be pronounced as th in *th*ese, but like the t-h in pen*t-h*ouse.

ড, ঢ. The English d and its corresponding aspirated letter. The sound of the latter is expressed by the d and h in ol*d-h*ouse. When written with a dot under them thus, ড়, ঢ়, they are pronounced as a lingual r and rh.

ণ has the same sound as n.

ত, থ. The dental t and its corresponding aspirated letter. The sound of the first of these letters is expressed in the provincial pronunciation of butter in Yorkshire.

দ, ধ. The dental d and its corresponding aspirated letter.

ন is pronounced as the English n.

প, ফ. P and its corresponding aspirated letter. The aspirated letter is pronounced like ph in ha*p-h*azard; and sometimes, though corruptly, like f.

ব, ভ, ম. B and its aspirate, and m.

য. This letter is properly the consonant y, but is pronounced like j, and sometimes, though improperly, like z. With a dot under it thus য়, and when compounded with a consonant, it expresses the sound of y.

র, ল, ব. The two first of these letters are r and l. The last is properly v or w. When not compounded, it is always pronounced as b; when compounded with another consonant, it has the sound of w.

শ, ষ, স. The natives make little or no distinction between these letters, though they belong to different organs. The two first ought to be pronounced nearly like sh, and the last like s.

হ is the English h.

ক্ষ is compounded of ক and ষ, but generally sounded like an aspirated k, with y*a* following it.

অ* sounds like aw at the beginning of a word, and generally like the short *u* in b*u*tter in the middle. It often, however, approaches to the sound of *o* in bottle.

---

* In expressing the vowels by English letters the following sounds are to be adhered to:

a sounds like a in father.
e - - like a in name, fame.
i - - like i in his, him.
i - - like i in time.
o - - like o in robe.
u - - like u in but, hut.
oo - - like oo in good.
oo - - like oo in rood.
y - - like y in you. This letter never has the sound of a vowel.

আ sounds as *a* in f*a*ther. This is accounted the long sound of the preceding letter.

ই, ঈ. The first of these letters sounds like *i* in h*i*s or h*i*m. The last like ee in sweet.

উ, ঊ. The first of these letters sounds like *oo* in g*oo*d; the last like oo in ooze.

ঋ, ৠ, are pronounced as *ri* in *ri*ch, and *ree* in *r*eed.

ঌ, ৡ. The first is pronounced as *li* in *li*ttle; the last like *l*ee in *l*eek.

এ, ঐ. The first of these letters sounds like a in name; the other, like *i* in t*i*me.

ও, ঔ. The sound of the first is that of o in cold; the other that of ow in owl.

ং, ঃ. The first of these characters is called *unooswur*, and sounds like *ung;* the other is called bis*urga*, and is pronounced like *uh*, ending very abruptly.

SECTION II.

Of Compounding Letters.

The vowel অ is inherent in every consonant; whenever, therefore, a consonant is followed by any other letter, that letter must be represented by a symbol which will occupy the place of the inherent vowel. *Exam.* কই must not be pronounced k*i* but k*ui*, and কর must not be pronounced kr*a*, but k*u*r*a*. To express k*i* and kr*a*, we must write কি and ক্র. This mark ্ under a letter denotes that the inherent vowel is suppressed.

Consonants may be compounded with vowels or with consonants. The compound letter thus formed is called ফলা or যুক্ত অক্ষর.

Of Compounding a Consonant with a Vowel.

1. A consonant when compounded with a vowel always precedes it.

2. The vowel অ being included in every consonant has no representative mark, it being sufficient to write the consonant. *Exam.* ক, k*a*, খ, kh*a*.

3. The other vowels are represented by the following symbols:

Vowel.	Symbol.	Compound.	Pronunciation.
আ	া	বা	ba.
ই	ি	বি	b*i*.
ঈ	ী	বী	bee.
উ	ু	বু	b*oo*.
ঊ	ূ	বূ	boo.
এ	ে	বে	be.
ঐ	ৈ	বৈ	bi.
ও	ো	বো	bo.
ঔ	ৌ	বৌ	bou.

4. Every consonant may take a vowel after it in the above manner. *Exam.* কি, k*i*; গী, gee; দে, de; হো, ho.

5. The consonant with its annexed vowel is esteemed one letter or rather syllable, and is pronounced as such. *Exam.* কি is not to be read k*u*-*i*, but k*i*. The junction of a consonant with a vowel is called বানান, or সিদ্ধি ফলা.

Of Compounding Consonants.

Two or more consonants may be joined so as to be pronounced without an intervening vowel. There are eleven regular forms of compounding consonants, viz.

6. Ky*a*-phola, or the junction of য with a preceding consonant. This is pronounced like y following the consonant, and is expressed by this character ্য. *Exam.* ক্য, খ্য, গ্য, ঘ্য; pronounced ky*a*, khy*a*, gy*a*, ghy*a*, with the y sounded as in *y*ou.

7. Kr*a*-phola, or the junction of র with a preceding consonant. This is expressed by ্র subjoined. *Exam.* ক্র, খ্র, গ্র, ঘ্র, kr*a*, khr*a*, gr*a*, ghr*a*.

8. Kn*a*-phola is ন subjoined. *Exam.* ক্ন, খ্ন, গ্ন, ঘ্ন, kn*a*, khn*a*, gn*a*, ghn*a*.

9. Kl*a*-phola is ল subjoined. *Exam.* ক্ল, খ্ল, গ্ল, ঘ্ল, kl*a*, khl*a*, gl*a*, ghl*a*.

10. Kw*a*-phola is ব subjoined. *Exam.* ক্ব, খ্ব, kw*a*, khw*a*. This is generally, though improperly, pronounced as if the consonant were doubled: thus, নিশ্বাস, generally pronounced n*i*shshas, should be pronounced n*i*shwas.

11. Km*a*-phola is ম subjoined. *Exam.* ক্ম, খ্ম, km*a*, khm*a*. This compound has two sounds, the one, which occurs when combined with ন, is very simple, as জন্ম, junm*a*; the other is a compound sound, as in আত্মা, পদ্ম, which cannot be expressed by English letters.

12. Kr*i*-phola is ঋ subjoined. It is expressed by this character ৃ. *Exam.* কৃ, খৃ, kr*i*, khr*i*.

13. Kl*i*-phola, or ৯ subjoined. *Exam.* কৢ, খৢ, kl*i*, khl*i*. This compound is seldom used.

14. Ark*a*-phola is the mark ʼ (substituted for র) placed over a consonant. In this compound the র must be pronounced first. *Exam.* দর্প, d*u*rp*a*.

15. Each nasal may be compounded with all the letters of its own class, and with no other; except that ঙ is compounded with all the অবর্গীয়, or miscellaneous letters. The compounds thus formed are called *U*nk*a*-phola.

N. B. The nasal is the first member of these compounds, which are thirty-three, viz.

ঙ্ক	ঙ্খ	ঙ্গ	ঙ্ঘ	ঙ্ঙ
ngk*a*	ngkh*a*	ng*a*	ngh*a*	nggn*a*
ঞ্চ	ঞ্ছ	ঞ্জ	ঞ্ঝ	ঞ্ঞ
nch*a*	nchh*a*	nj*a*	njh*a*	nggn*a*
ণ্ট	ণ্ঠ	ণ্ড	ণ্ঢ	ণ্ণ
nṭ*a*	nṭh*a*	nḍ*a*	nḍh*a*	nṇ*a*
ন্ত	ন্থ	ন্দ	ন্ধ	ন্ন
nt*a*	nth*a*	nd*a*	ndh*a*	nn*a*

ম্প	ম্ফ	ম্ব	ম্ভ	ম্ম
mp*a*	mph*a*	mb*a*	mbh*a*	mm*a*
ঞ্জ	——	ঙ্ল	ঙ্ব	——
nj*a*	——	ngl*a*	ngw*a*	——
ঙ্শ	ঙ্ষ	ঙ্স	ঙ্হ	ঙ্ক্ষ
ngsh*a*	ngsh*a*	ngs*a*	ngh*a*	ngkhy*a*

16. *U*ska-phola is the composition of শ, ষ, and স, with other letters of the same organ. It comprizes a few other compounds, making in all thirty-three, viz.

স্ক	স্খ	দ্গ	দ্ঘ	ঙ্ষ্ট্র
sk*a*	skh*a*	dg*a*	dgh*a*	ngstr*a*
শ্চ	শ্ছ	ব্জ	ব্ঝ	জ্ঞ
shch*a*	shchh*a*	bj*a*	bjh*a*	ggy*a*
ষ্ট	ষ্ঠ	ব্ড	ব্ঢ	ষ্ণ
st*a*	sth*a*	bd*a*	bdh*a*	shn*a*
স্ত	স্থ	ব্দ	ব্ধ	হ্ন
st*a*	sth*a*	bd*a*	bdh*a*	hn*a*
স্প	স্ফ	দ্ব	দ্ভ	হ্ম
sp*a*	sph*a*	db*a*	dbh*a*	hm*a*
হ্য	——	হ্ল	হ্ব	——
hj*a*	——	hl*a*	hw*a*	——
ট্শ	ট্ষ	ট্স	ট্হ	ট্ক্ষ
tsh*a*	tsh*a*	ts*a*	th*a*	tkhy*a*

17. All the letters may be doubled, as ক্ক, চ্চ, ন্ন, &c. When an aspirated letter is doubled, the first member is changed for its corresponding unaspirated letter, as চ্ছ, ক্খ, &c.

18. Though ঋ and ঌ are vowels, yet their combinations are reckoned among those of the consonants, and not

in the banan*a*, or combination of a consonant with a vowel.

19. The following are Contractions, some used for elegance, others for expedition:

ক্র, kr*a*.
ক্ত, kt*a*
কু, k*oo*.
মু, m*oo*.
ত্ত, tt*a* and t*oo*. It ought never to be used for the latter.
গু, g*oo*.
শু, sh*oo*.
হু, h*oo*.
ত্র, tr*a*.
ত্ত্র, ttr*a*.
হৃ, hr*i*.
হ্র, hr*a*.
রু, রূ, roo, r*oo*.
হ্ন, hn*a*.
হ্য, hj*a*.
স্তু, st*oo*.
স্ত্র, str*a*.
গ্ধ, gdh*a*.
ৎ, t.
শ্রী, shree.
৭, g*u*nesh, (the name of a H*i*nd*oo* god.)
৺, eeshw*u*r*a*, or lord.

20. ু this mark on the right side of any letter signifies উ if turned upwards, and ঊ if turned downwards.

21. placed over a vowel, represents the nasal, which properly coalesces with the following consonant, and gives the letter over which it is placed a strong nasal sound.

N. B. Every one who wishes to learn the Bengalee language should make himself perfectly acquainted with the characters and their powers before he proceeds any further. A superficial knowledge of these generally occasions a vicious pronunciation, which is with difficulty corrected.

SECTION III.

Of Words.

1. WORDS are divided into nouns, verbs, and indeclinable particles.

2. Nouns are distinguished into দ্রব্যবাচক, substantives, or names of things; গুনবাচক, names of qualities, or adjectives; and অনুকরণ শব্দ, imitative sounds. Some of these sounds are substantives, others are adjectives, and others adverbs.

3. Substantives are further divided into নামবাচক, proper names, জাতিবাচক, generic names, and ভাববাচক, abstract nouns; these are of two sorts, viz. ভাববাচক, names of abstract ideas, and ক্রিয়াবাচক, verbal nouns.

4. Nouns are also further distinguished into প্রাণীবাচক, names of animals, and অপ্রাণিবাচক, names of inanimate things.

5. The most useful distribution of words is into বিশেষণ, discriminating words, and বিশিষ্য, words to be discriminated; the first are adjectives, adverbs, &c. which express the quality or circumstance of a thing or action, and the last the thing or action itself.

Of Substantives.

There are but two declensions of nouns; the difference between those ending with a consonant, and those ending with a vowel, being too inconsiderable to require that a distinction should be made in their declension.

There are seven cases: the Nominative, Accusative, Instrumental, Dative, Ablative, Possessive, and Locative, which, answering to the *Sungskrita* cases, are placed in the same order as in that language. When merely enumerated they are called প্রথম, *the first*, দ্বিতীয়, *the second*, তৃতীয়, *the third*, চতুর্থ, *the fourth*, পঞ্চম, *the fifth*, ষষ্ঠ, *the sixth*, and সপ্তম, *the seventh.* When considered as in construction with verbs, they are called কর্ত্তা, *the agent*; কর্ম্ম, *the object*; করণ, *the instrument*; সম্প্রদান, *the giving*; অপাদান, *the withdrawing*; সম্বন্ধ, *the connecting*; and অধিকরণ, *the possessing* form.

6. There are two numbers, the singular (একবচন), and the plural (বহুবচন). *Exam.* জন, *a man*, জনেরা, *men.*

7. There are three genders (লিঙ্গ); the masculine (পুং লিঙ্গ), the feminine (স্ত্রীলিঙ্গ), and the neuter (ক্লীব or নপুংসকলিঙ্গ.) *Exam.* পুরুষ, *a male*, নারী, *a woman*, জ্ঞান, *knowledge.*

8. In masculine and feminine nouns, the different cases are formed by affixing the following inflective terminations (বিভক্তি), which serve equally for the singular and plural numbers, viz. for the Accusative কে, for the Instrumental তে, for the Dative রে, for the Ablative তে or হইতে, for the Possessive or Genitive র, and for the Locative এ or তে. The এ of the locative case never follows a vowel.

9. If the word end in a consonant, এ must be inserted before the terminations, the accusative termination কে, and the locative এ excepted: if the word have a final অ, the inserted এ and the locative termination এ must occupy its place. *Exam.* মনুষ্যেতে, *by a man*, মনুষ্যকে, *man*, মনুষ্যে, *in a man.*

The Dative is optionally made by কে, like the accusative. *Exam.* দাসেরে, or দাসকে, *to a servant.*

10. য় is optionally substituted for the termination এ of the locative case, when the word has a final আ. *Exam.* পিতায়, পিতাতে, *in the father.*

11. The nominative plural is formed by affixing রা, or রান্, to the word; এ must be inserted before it unless the word have a final vowel. *Exam.* অশ্বেরা, or অশ্বেরান্, *horses;* গরুরা, or গরুরান্, *cows.*

12. To make the plural, the syllable দিগ্, is inserted before the terminations of all the cases except the nominatives; এ must be inserted after দিগ, in all cases, except when followed by the কে of the accusative, and the এ of the locative case. *Exam.* দাসেরদিগেতে, *by servants;* দাসেরদিগকে, *servants;* দাসেরদিগে, *among servants.*

13. ব্ is optionally inserted before the syllable দিগ. If the word end in অ or a consonant, এ must be inserted before ব্ when thus introduced. *Exam.* দাসেরদিগেরে, দাস দিগেরে, *to servants;* দাসীরদিগেরে, দাসীদিগেরে, *to female servants.*

14. দিগ্ is optionally inserted in the genitive plural. *Exam.* বন্ধুরদের, বন্ধুরদিগের, *of relations.*

দের is optionally substituted for the inserted syllable দিগ্ in the ablative and possessive plural. When this substitution takes place in the possessive, the termination of the case is suppressed. *Exam.* মনুষ্যেরদেরহইতে, or মনুষ্যেরদিগ হইতে, *from men;* মনুষ্যেরদের, and মনুষ্যেরদিগের, *men.*

15. Words which in Sungskrita have a final ইন্, end in ঈ in the Bengalee language. The final long vowel of these words becomes short when the word is declined. *Exam.* আজ্ঞাকারী, *a commander*, আজ্ঞাকারিতে, *by a commander.*

Example of a Regular Noun.

Masc. or *Fem.*

	Sing.	Plur.
N.	কুকুর, *a dog.*	কুকুরেরা, কুকুরেরান্, *dogs.*
Ac.	কুকুরকে, *dog.*	কুকুরেরদিগকে, *dogs.*
I.	কুকুরতে, *by a dog.*	কুকুরের্দিগেতে, *by dogs.*
D.	কুকুরেরে, *to a dog.*	কুকুরের্দিগেরে, *to dogs.*
A.	কুকুরেতে, কুকুরহইতে, *from a dog.*	কুকুরেরদিগেতে, কুকুরের দিগ্হইতে, কুকুরেরদের হইতে, *from dogs.*

	Sing.	Plur.
P.	কুকুরের, *a dog's.*	কুকুরেরদের, কুকুরেরদিগের, *dogs'.*
L.	কুকুরে, কুকুরেতে, *in a dog.*	কুকুরের্দিগেতে, *in dogs.*

Of Neuter Nouns.

16. Neuter nouns have no plural, unless they are personified. In that case they lose their neuter signification, and become either masculine or feminine. *Exam.* দুঃখী জন বৃক্ষেরদিগকে কথা কহিল, *the afflicted man spoke to the trees.*

The following is an example of the Declension of a noun with a final vowel.

Masculine.

	Sing.	Plur.
N.	প্রভু, *a lord.*	প্রভুরা, *lords.*
Ac.	প্রভুকে, *lord.*	প্রভুরদিগকে, *lords.*
I.	প্রভুতে, *by a lord.*	প্রভুরদিগেতে, *by lords.*
D.	প্রভুরে, *to a lord.*	প্রভুরদিগেরে, *to lords.*
A.	প্রভুতে, প্রভুহইতে, *from a lord.*	প্রভুরদিগেতে, প্রভুরদিগহইতে প্রভুরদেরহইতে, *from lords.*
P.	প্রভুর, *a lord's.*	প্রভুরদের, প্রভুরদিগের, *lords'.*
L.	প্রভুতে, *in a lord.*	প্রভুরদিগেতে, *in or among lords.*

Nouns ending in আ are declined thus:

Sing.

N. পিতা, *a father.*
Ac. পিতাকে, *father.*
I. পিতাতে, *by a father.*
D. পিতারে, *to a father.*

A. পিতাতে, পিতাহইতে, *from a father.*
P. পিতার্, *father's.*
L. পিতায়, পিতাতে, *in a father.*
The plural as প্রভু.

17. Neuters are inflected by the following বিভক্তি, or terminations, viz. Instrumental এ, or তে; Dative এ, or তে; Ablative এ, তে, or হইতে; Possessive or Genitive র্; and Locative এ, or তে. The Accusative is the same as the Nominative.

Sing. and Plur.

N. হাত, *a hand.*
Ac. হাত, *hand.*
I. হাতে, and হাতেতে, *by a hand.*
D. হাতে, and হাতেতে, *to a hand.*
A. হাতে, হাতেতে, and হাতহইতে, *from a hand.*
P. হাতের্, *of a hand.*
L. হাতে, and হাতেতে, *in a hand.*

18. Common nouns are declined like masculines or feminines.

19. গুণ, or গুলা is often affixed to neuter nouns, to express the plural number: it is also sometimes inserted between the noun and the inflection in masculines and feminines signifying brute animals, to distinguish them as inferior to men.

Sing. and Plur.

N. হাঁড়ি, *a pot.*
Ac. হাঁড়ি, *pot.*
I. হাঁড়িতে, *by a pot.*

D. হাঁড়িতে, *to a pot.*
A. হাঁড়িতে, and হাঁড়িহইতে, *from a pot.*
P. হাঁড়ির, *of a pot.*
L. হাঁড়িতে, *in a pot.*

Sing. and Plur.

N. মৃত্তিকা, *earth.*
Ac. মৃত্তিকা, *earth.*
I. মৃত্তিকাতে, *by earth.*
D. মৃত্তিকাতে, *to earth.*
A. মৃত্তিকাতে, মৃত্তিকাহইতে, *from earth.*
P. মৃত্তিকার, *of earth.*
L. মৃত্তিকায়, মৃত্তিকাতে, *in earth.*

Observations of the Nouns.

20. When a person goes to a place by some particular road, or through some town or other intermediate place the participles হইয়া, or দিয়া, are constructed with the nouns instead of the termination of the third case. *Exam.* আমি শ্রীরামপুর হইয়া or দিয়া কলিকাতায় গেলাম, *I went by* or *through Serampore to Calcutta.*

21. When the means of accomplishing any thing is compared in the mind to a way, the instrumental is often expressed by the participles দিয়া, or করিয়া. The simple instrumental noun is also often expressed in the same manner. *Exam.* আমি আপনার হাত দিয়া করিয়াছি *I did it with my own hand.* আমি কেমন করিয়া তাহা করিব *how shall I do it?*

22. When a thing is accomplished by means of some intervening circumstance, or person, the third case is op-

tionally expressed by দ্বারা, which is the Sungskrita instrumental case of দ্বার, *a door. Exam.* তদ্দ্বারা or তাহাতে তোমার অনুগ্রহ পাইয়াছি, *I obtained your favour through him, or it.*

23. When a thing is accomplished by some instrument, the third case is optionally expressed by compounding the word with করণ, *a doing;* ক must be affixed to this compound. *Exam.* আমি কলমকরণক or কলমেতে লিখি, *I write with a pen.*

24. The third case is used when an action is represented as done by the agent of a passive verb; this sense is also expressed by compounding the word with কর্ত্তৃ, *an agent;* ক must be affixed to this compound. *Exam* ঈশ্বরেতে or ঈশ্বরকর্ত্তৃক জগৎ সৃষ্ট ছিল, *the world was created by God.*

25. The third case is employed when a thing is said to be done by the intervention of some predisposing circumstance: this sense may also be expressed by compounding the word with পূর্ব্ব, *before;* ক must be affixed to this compound. *Exam.* আপনকার অনুগ্রহেতে or অনুগ্রহপূর্ব্বক কর্ম্ম সিদ্ধ হইল, *the business was accomplished by your kindness.*

26. The instrumental case is sometimes expressed by the ablative form in হইতে, when an action is performed by the agent of a passive verb. *Exam.* তোমাহইতে গুরুর এবং পুত্রের প্রাণ রক্ষা হইল, *the preservation of my preceptor's and of my son's life was effected by thee.*

27. All the words and particles by which the instrumental case is expressed are affixed to the word, or its sub-

stitute, in the same manner as the inflective terminations; sometimes, however, though it is manifestly improper, except in the instance of দ্বারা, they govern the possessive case. *Exam.* তদ্দ্বারা or তাহার দ্বারা পাইয়াছি, *I obtained it through him.*

28. The ablative of masculine and feminine nouns is optionally made by compounding or constructing the word with ঠাঁই, or স্থান, *a place,* or with কাছ, *a shore, vicinity;* স্থান, and কাছ, are in this instance put in the ablative case. *Exam.* তাহাতে, তাহাহইতে, তাহার কাছ, তাহার কাছহইতে, তাহার ঠাঁই, তাহার স্থানে or তাহার স্থানহইতে আমি পাইয়াছি, *I obtained it from him.* তাহার মুখেতে or মুখহইতে শাপবাণী নির্গত হইতেছিল, *the curse was proceeding from her mouth.*

29. Such English phrases as, "the darkness of distress," "the waters of affliction," &c. are usually expressed by compounding রূপ, *a form,* with the word which would otherwise be in the possessive case. *Exam.* শোকরূপ অন্ধকার, *the darkness of distress.* দুর্গতিরূপ জল, *the waters of affliction.* The possessive case would be improper here, because darkness and water are not things belonging to, or possessed by grief or affliction, but figurative expressions denoting them.

30. The locative case is optionally expressed by either compounding or constructing the word with the words মধ্য or মাঝ, *the midst.* These words must in this instance be in the locative case. *Exam.* তাহারদের মধ্যে or মাঝে *among them.* তন্মধ্যে or তাহার মধ্যে, *in it.*

31. The vocative (সম্বোধন) is not reckoned a distinct

case, but only a particular modification of the Nominative case.

In the vocative, এ is substituted for the final of words ending in ই, and ও for that of words ending in উ. The vocative of feminines with a final আ is made by the substitution of এ for it. *Exam.* হরে, *O Huri.* প্রভো, *O Lord.* প্রিয়ে, *O beloved.*

The vocative case is usually preceded by the particles গো, ভো, হে, রে, লো, টে, টি, গে, হারে, or হেরে.

গো is used in addressing parents, teachers, an elder brother, or any person to whom we intend respect.

ভো is seldom used, but is indiscriminately applied to all genders.

হে is used in addressing an equal: and রে a familiar friend, or an inferior.

লো is used in addressing an inferior woman, টে a young woman, and টি a child.

গে is used only in the north of Bengal.

হারে or হেরে is used in addressing common or inferior people.

32. When the person called to is at a distance, but within sight, the vocative particle is preceded by ও, আ, or এ. *Exam.* ওগো মাতা, *O mother.* ওগো পিতা, *O father.* ওহে রাম, *O Rama.* আরে, ওরে, or এরে ছোক্রা, *O boy.*

ওলো মাগী, *O woman.* ওগো মাতা, *O mother.* ওটে দাসী, *O handmaid.* ওটি ছুক্রী, *O girl.* If the person be very distant, the ও is much lengthened.

When the person or thing is present, the sign of the vocative frequently follows the proper name. *Exam.* বাবাগো, *O father.* মাগো, *O mother.* দাদাগো, *O elder brother.* মাসীগো, *O aunt.* রামহে, *O Rama.* গোলোকহে, *O Goluka.* মুটিয়ারে, *O labourer.* গোয়ালারে, *O cow-keeper.* পদ্মরে, *O Pudma.*

33. The vocative particle is often constructed with an interrogatory sentence. *Exam.* তুমি কেন বল না গো? *why do you not speak, Sir?* তুই কেন বলিস না রে? *why dost thou not speak?* কেন গো বল না? *why do you not speak, Sir?* কেন রে বলিস না? *why dost thou not speak?*

34. The vocative particle is often joined to the imperative verb. *Exam.* খাও গো, *eat, Sir.* কর হে, *do it.* বল রে, *speak.*

Of the Gender of Nouns.

35. Names of male animals are masculine, those of females feminine, and those of all other things neuter.

36. The feminine of common nouns, and of masculines, ending either with a consonant or অ, is made by affixing আ or ঈ. Some feminines require the lengthening of the vowel which precedes the termination. *Exam.* নর, *a man,* নারী, *a woman.* পুত্র, *a son,* পুত্রী, *a daughter.* তনয়, *a son,* তনয়া, *a daughter.*

The feminine of words ending in অক is made by affixing আ. ই must in this case be inserted before the final ক. *Exam.* পালক, *nourisher,* পালিকা, *a female nourisher.* লেখক, *a writer,* লেখিকা, *a female writer.*

37. Names of animals ending with a vowel usually make the feminine in ঈ.

Examples.

Masc.	Fem.
বাঘ, *a tyger.*	বাঘী, and বাঘিনী.
বিড়াল, *a cat.*	বিড়ালী.
কাক, *a crow.*	কাকী.
বুলবুল, *a bulbul.*	বুলবুলী.
হরিণ, *a deer.*	হরিণী.
মৃগ, *a deer.*	মৃগী.
গাধা, *an ass.*	গাধী.
ভেড়া, *a sheep.*	ভেড়ী.

The feminine of those words ending in ঈ, which in S*ungskrita* have a final ইন্, is constantly made by affixing ঈ to the original S*ungskrita* form of the masculine. *Exam.* হস্তিনী, *a female elephant,* পক্ষিণী, *a female bird.*

38. Many words ending in উ or ঊ do not admit these terminations, but are distinguished by the words পুরুষ, *male,* and স্ত্রী, *female.*

39. The feminine of some words with a final তি is made by substituting ত্নী for the final syllable. *Exam.* হাতি, *an elephant,* হাত্নী, *a female elephant.* পতি, *a lord or husband,* পত্নী, *a wife.*

The following feminines are irregular:

Masc.	Fem.
পুরুষ, *a man.*	স্ত্রী, *a woman.*
পুরুষ, *spirit or the creating power.*	প্রকৃতী, *plastic matter.*
পিতা, *a father.*	মাতা, *a mother.*
বাপ, *a father.*	মা, *a mother.*
ভ্রাতা, *a brother.*	ভগিনী, *a sister.*
ভাই, *a brother.*	বহিনী, or বুন, *a sister.*
হোলা, *a he-cat.*	মেচী, *a she cat.*
শুক, *a species of parrot.*	শারী, *the female parrot.*
মদনা, *a species of parrot.*	কাজলা, *the female parrot.*
আঁড়িয়া, *a bull.*	গাই, *a cow.*
রাজা, *a king.*	রাণী, *a queen.*

Of Enclitic Particles.

40. The words টা and গোটা, *whole,* খান, *a piece,* টুকি, *a little,* গুলা, গুলিন্ and গুল, *a ball,* or *a lump,* are in many instances compounded with words in the manner of enclitic particles, but they never throw the accent forward. These words are often thus constructed with nouns and pronouns, and with adjectives, when put absolutely, or in the place of substantives.

41. When any one asks another for a number of articles, without saying how many, গোটা is introduced as the first word of the sentence. *Exam.* গোটা তিনেক দেও, *give me about three.*

If the article wanted be specified, the name is generally put first. *Exam.* আম গোটা তিনেক দেও, *give me about three mangoes.*

If the number be mentioned precisely, টা must be added instead of গোটা. *Exam.* দশটা আম দেও, *give me ten mangoes.*

42. টা is added, first, to nouns which signify uncompounded substances, as fruits and vegetables; secondly, to names of animals; thirdly, to names of vessels which have their sides raised up, such as bottles, cups, pitchers, jars, &c.; fourthly, to the names of complete substances, and other things which are composed of several subordinate parts; fifthly, to the names of almost all the members of the body; sixthly, to all numerals; and seventhly, to all the pronouns, except আমি, মুই, তুমি and তুই. *Exam.* পেয়ালাটা, *a cup;* পেয়ারাটা *a guava;* কুকুরটা, *a dog;* বাটীটা, *a house,* (including all its offices); সিন্ধুকটা, *a chest;* অঙ্গুলিটা, *a finger.*

43. খান is added, first, to the names of all vessels which are flat or nearly so, such as plates, saucers, &c. also to bricks and tiles; secondly, to the names of weapons and working tools, except বর্চি, *a spear,* বন্দুক, *a gun,* তীর, *an arrow,* and a few others; thirdly, to the names of the subordinate parts of compounded substances; and fourthly, to হাত, *a hand,* পা, *a foot,* and মুখ, *a face.* *Exam.* পিরিজখান, *a saucer;* ঘরখান, *a single house or office belonging to a homestead;* ডালাখান, *the cover of a chest;* হাতখান, *a hand.*

44. ডা is often joined to pronouns, and to nouns signifying animals, instead of টা. *Exam.* পুত্রডা, *a son.*

45. জন, *a man,* is frequently put before nouns signifying men. টা is only used after such words in a dimi-

nutive sense. *Exam.* দশ জন মজুরকে ডাক, *call ten labourers.*

46. ডি and টি are affixed to words signifying young persons, and to those which signify inferior animals when we design to express affection or pity towards them. *Exam.* ছালিয়াটি সুবুদ্ধি বটে, *the child is docile, truly.* আমার বড় পুত্রডির বিবাহ দিব, *I will give my eldest son in marriage.*

47. গুলা, গুলি, গুলু and গুলিন্, are affixed to plural nouns. গুলিন and গুলু are rather more respectful than গুলা, and are used when affection or pity towards man or inferior animals is to be expressed. *Exam.* তাহার অনেক গুলিন্ সন্তান, *he had many children.*

48. গণ, *a genus,* জাতি, *a tribe or sort,* বর্গ, *a class,* and দল, *an army, a band,* are often added to nouns which signify animals. *Exam.* রাজাগণ উঠিয়া গেলেন, *the princes rose and departed.* বানর পশুজাতি সে কি জানে, *the monkey is a beast; what does he know?* ভৃত্যবর্গেরা আজ্ঞা পাইয়া ক্রিয়া করিল, *the servants having received the order, did the business.* কুরুদল, *a band of Kooroos.*

49. লোক, *a person,* is compounded with words signifying men. *Exam.* সাহেবলোক, *gentlemen.* মজুরলোক, *labourers.*

When লোক, *a world,* is compounded with দেব, *a god,* মনুষ্য, *a man,* নাগ, *a serpent,* and with several other words of the same meaning, it signifies the place inhabited by them. *Exam.* দেবলোক, *heaven.* নরলোক, *the earth.* নাগ লোক, patala, or *the lower regions.*

50. টুকি, *a little,* and খানিক, *some,* are affixed to words meaning fluid substances, and to pulverized substances which move somewhat in the manner of fluids, such as ধুলা, *dust,* কর্দ্দম, *mud.* *Exam.* জলটুকি তাহাকে দেও, *give him a little water.* খানিক দুগ্ধ ছিল, *there was a little milk.*

51. গুচ্ছার, *some,* is added to the names of crumbled substances, to rice or other grain, and to words signifying straw, grass, &c. *Exam.* চাউল গুচ্ছার দেও, *give me some rice.* খড় গুচ্ছার দেও, *give me some straw.*

SECTION IV.

Of Adjectives, (গুণবাচক.)

1. Adjectives have no variation of case or number, unless they stand in an absolute form, and answer the purpose of substantives. *Exam.* সে ক্ষুদ্রের, *that little (person's or thing's.)*

2. The genders are distinguished in the same manner as those of nouns substantive. *Exam.* সুন্দর, *beautiful,* fem. সুন্দরী.

3. The masculine of adjectives with a final বৎ and মৎ is made by substituting বান্ for the final বৎ, and মান্ for the final মৎ. The feminine of both is made by affixing ঈ to the বৎ or মৎ. *Exam.* Neut. রূপবৎ, masc. রূপবান, fem. রূপবতী, *beautiful.* Neut. বুদ্ধিমৎ, masc. বুদ্ধিমান, fem. বুদ্ধিমতী, *wise.*

4. The feminine of almost all adjectives ending in অ is made by আ, and that of the greater part of those which end in a consonant, and of some which end in অ or ই, is made by ঈ. *Exam.* বিভিন্ন, *separated,* fem. বিভিন্না. দত্ত, *given,* fem. দত্তা. সুন্দর, *beautiful,* fem. সুন্দরী.

5. The final অক্ of an adjective is usually changed to ইকা, to make the feminine. *Exam.* কারক, *doing,* fem. কারিকা.

6. Sungskrita adjectives with a final ইন্ end with ঈ Bengalee. The feminine of these is made by affixing ঈ

the Sungskrita form. *Exam.* কারী, *doing,. acting,* fem. কারিনী. দর্শী, *seeing,* fem. দর্শিনী.

Of the Comparison of Adjectives.

7. Adjectives are compared by adding তর for the comparative, and তম for the superlative. *Exam.* প্রিয়, *beloved;* প্রিয়তর, *more beloved;* প্রিয়তম, *best beloved.*

8. The degrees of comparison are most commonly made by prefixing আর, *more,* to make the comparative, and অতি, or অত্যন্ত, *very, exceedingly,* to form the superlative. *Exam.* শক্ত, *strong,* আর শক্ত, *stronger,* অতিশক্ত or অত্যন্ত শক্ত, *most* or *exceedingly strong.*

9. A great number of adjectives are apparently formed at pleasure, by affixing ই or ইয়া to imitative sounds, which are composed of two members, neither of which has any meaning singly; as ঠন্ঠনী, *rebounding;* টল্মলী, *unsteady, like a boat on rough water;* চট্পটিয়া, *constantly moving, like a person in a fever;* চক্মকিয়া, *glittering;* ঝন্ঝনী, *sounding like falling rain;* আঁকুবাঁকু, *hastily;* এলুমেলু *confused, disordered.*

SECTION V.

Of Pronouns, (সর্ব্বনাম.)

1. Pronouns have the masculine, feminine, and neuter genders. They are declined like nouns.

2. There are two kinds of personal pronouns, the one used to express superiority or honour, the other inferiority or contempt. The honorific (গৌরবোক্তি) pronouns are আমি, *I*; তুমি, *thou*; তিনি,* তিঁহ,* and তিনি,* *he*; ইনি,† ঞিহ,† ইহ,† and উহ,† *this man*; উনি,‡ উঁহ,‡ and উহ,‡ *that man*, (viz. *that man to whom I point*;) যিনি, *who*, and আপনি, *self*. Those denoting inferiority (নীচোক্তি) are মুই, *I*; তুই, *thou*; সে, *he*; এ, *this person* or *thing*; ঐ or ও, *that person* or *thing*. যে, *who*, and কে, *who?* তিঁহ, তিহ, তিনি, উঁহ, উহ, ইঁহ, and ইহ, are seldom used in the nominative case.

3. আপনি may be joined to any other personal pronoun. *Exam.* আমি আপনি, *I myself.* তিনি আপনি, *he himself.*

4. When আপনি governs a verb of the first person, it means *I myself*; but its most common use is to address a superior, which, in the polite or respectful style, is generally done in the third person. Thus, আপনি তাহা করিয়াছেন, *your honour has done it.*

* These pronouns are used when the person spoken of is absent.

† These are used when the person is present.

‡ These are used when the person is present, but at some distance.

আমি, *I.*

5. In declining this pronoun, আমা is substituted for আমি, in all the cases except the nominative singular. আম্ is substituted for it in the nominative plural.

6. The final ই is rejected before the termination of the nominative plural in the first and second personal pronouns.

	Sing.	Plur.
N.	আমি, *I.*	আম্‌রা, *we.*
Ac.	আমাকে, *me.*	আমার্‌দিগ্‌কে, *us.*
I.	আমাতে, *by me.*	আমার্‌দিগেতে, *by us.*
D.	আমারে, *to me.*	আমার্‌দিগেরে, *to us.*
A.	আমাতে, আমাহইতে, *from me.*	আমার্‌দিগেতে, আমার্‌দের্ হইতে, আমার্‌দিগ্‌হইতে, *from us.*
P.	আমার্, *my.*	আমার্‌দের, আমার্‌দিগের, *our.*
L.	আমায়, *in me.*	আমার্‌দিগেতে, *in us.*

মুই, *I.*

7. মো is substituted for মুই, in all the cases except the nominative singular.

	Sing.	Plur.
N.	মুই, *I.*	মোরা, *we.*
Ac.	মোকে, *me.*	মোর্‌দিগ্‌কে, *us.*
I.	মোতে, *by me.*	মোর্‌দিগেতে, *by us.*
D.	মোরে, *to me.*	মোর্‌দিগেরে, *to us.*
A.	মোতে, মোহইতে, *from me.*	মোর্‌দিগেতে, মোর্‌দের্‌হইতে, and মোর্‌দিগ্‌হইতে, *from us.*
P.	মোর্, *my.*	মোর্‌দের্, মোর্‌দিগের, *our.*
L.	মোতে, *in me.*	মোরদিগেতে, *in us.*

তুমি, *thou.*

8. তোমা is substituted for তুমি in all the cases except the nominative singular. তোম্ is substituted for it in the nominative plural.

9. ও is substituted for the উ of তুমি, in the nominative plural.

	Sing.	Plur.
N.	তুমি, *thou.*	তোম্‌রা, *ye or you.*
Ac.	তোমাকে, *thee.*	তোমার্‌দিগ্‌কে, *you.*
I.	তোমাতে, *by thee.*	তোমার্‌দিগেতে, *by you.*
D.	তোমারে, *to thee.*	তোমার্‌দিগেরে, *to you.*
A.	তোমাতে, তোমাহই তে, *from thee.*	তোমার্‌দিগেতে, তোমার্‌দের্‌হইতে, তোমার্‌দিগ্‌হইতে, *from you.*
P.	তোমার, *thy.*	তোমার্‌দের, তোমার্‌দিগের, *yours.*
L.	তোমায়, *in thee.*	তোমার্‌দিগেতে, *in you.*

10. তো is substituted for তুই, *thou,* (inferior) in all cases except the nominative singular. It is declined like মুই.

তিনি *he.*

11. তেনা and তাহা are substituted for তিনি in all cases except the nominative singular.

	Sing.	Plur.
N.	তিনি, *he.*	তাহারা, তেনারা, *they.*
Ac.	তাহাকে, তেনাকে, *him.*	তাহারদিগকে, তেনার্‌দিগ্‌কে, *them.*
I.	তাহাতে, তেনাতে, *by him.*	তাহার্‌দিগেতে, তেনার্‌দিগে তে, *by them.*

	Sing.	Plur.
D.	তাহারে, তেনারে, *to him.*	তাহার্‌দিগেরে, তেনার্‌দিগেরে, *to them.*
A.	তাহাতে, তাহাহইতে, তেনাতে, তেনাহইতে, *from him.*	তাহার্‌দিগেতে, তাহার্‌দেরহইতে, তাহার্‌দিগ্‌হইতে, তেনার্‌দিগেতে, তেনার্‌দের হইতে, তেনার্‌দিগ্‌হইতে, *from them.*
P.	তাহার, তেনার, *his.*	তাহার্‌দের, তাহারদিগের, তেনারদের, তেনার্‌দিগের, *their.*
L.	তাহায়, তেনায়, *in him.*	তাহার্‌দিগেতে, তেনার্‌দিগেতে, *in them.*

Thus, সিনি, *he,* substituting সেনা in the oblique cases.

তিহ, *he.*

12. তাহা is substituted for তিহ, *he,* in the oblique cases.

	Sing.	Plur.
N.	তিহ, *he.*	তাহারা, *they.*
Ac.	তাহাকে, *him.*	তাহার্‌দিগ্‌কে, *them.*
I.	তাহাতে, *by him.*	তাহার্‌দিগেতে, *by them.*
D.	তাহারে, *to him.*	তাহার্‌দিগেরে, *to them.*
A.	তাহাতে, তাহাহইতে, *from him.*	তাহার্‌দিগেতে, তাহার্‌দের্‌ হইতে, তাহার্‌দিগ্‌হইতে, *from them.*
P.	তাহার, *his.*	তাহার্‌দের, তাহার্‌দিগের, *their.*
L.	তাহায়, *in him.*	তাহার্‌দিগেতে, *in them.*

Thus তিঁহ, *he,* (very honorific), substituting তাঁহা in all the cases except the nominative singular.

ইনি, *this man.*

13. ইনা and ইহা are substituted for ইনি in all the cases except the nominative singular.

	Sing.	Plur.
N.	ইনি, *he.*	ইহারা, ইনারা, *they.*
Ac.	ইহাকে, ইনাকে, *him.*	ইহার্দিগ্কে, ইনার্দিগ্কে *them.*
I.	ইহাতে, ইনাতে, *by him.*	ইহার্দিগেতে, ইনার্দিগেতে *by them.*
D.	ইহারে, ইনারে, *to him.*	ইহার্দিগেরে, ইনার্দিগেরে, *to them.*
A.	ইহাতে, ইনাতে, ইহাহইতে, ইনাহইতে, *from him.*	ইহার্দিগেতে, ইহার্দেরহইতে, ইহার্দিগ্হইতে, ইনার্দিগেতে, ইনার্দেরহইতে, ইনার্দিগ্হইতে, *from them.*
P.	ইহার, ইনার, *his.*	ইহার্দের, ইহার্দিগের, ইনার্দের, ইনার্দিগের, *their.*
L.	ইহায়, ইনায়, *in him.*	ইহার্দিগেতে, ইনার্দিগেতে, *in them.*

Thus, উনি, *that man,* substituting উনা and উহা in all the cases except the nominative singular.

ইহ্, *this man.*

14. ইহা is substituted for ইহ্ in all the cases except the nominative singular.

	Sing.	Plur.
N.	ইহ্, *he.*	ইহা, *they.*

Ac.	ইহাকে, *him.*	ইহার্দিগ্কে, *them.*
I.	ইহাতে, *by him.*	ইহার্দিগেতে, *by them.*
D.	ইহারে, *to him.*	ইহার্দিগেরে, *to them.*
A.	ইহাতে, ইহাহইতে, *from him.*	ইহার্দিগেতে, ইহারদেরহইতে, ইহার্দিগ্হইতে, *from them.*
P.	ইহার, *his.*	ইহারদের, ইহার্দিগের, *their.*
L.	ইহায়, *in him.*	ইহার্দিগেতে, *in them.*

Thus also are declined ইঁহ, *this man*, উহ and উঁহ, *that man*, substituting respectively ইঁহা, উহা, and উঁহা.

15. আপনা is substituted for আপনি, *self.* যেনা and যাহা are substituted for the relative pronoun যিনি, *what man. Exam.* আপনারে, *to self,* যেনাতে or যাহাতে, by *whom.*

16. The inferior pronouns, এ, *this* (*man, woman* or *thing*), ও, *that* (*man, woman* or *thing*), সে, *that* (*absent man, woman* or *thing*), যে, *what* (*man, woman* or *thing*), কে, *who?* and কেহ, *any one*, are respectively changed for ইহা, উহা, তা or তাহা, যা or যাহা, কা or কাহা, in all the cases except the nominative singular, সে, তা, and তাহা, *that*, and যে, যা, যাহা, *what*, are the neuter pronouns.

সে, *he, she* or *it.*

Masculine and Feminine.

	Sing.	Plur.
N.	সে, *he.*	তাহারা, *they.*
Ac.	তাহাকে, *him.*	তাহার্দিগ্কে, *them.*
I.	তাহাতে, *by him.*	তাহার্দিগেতে, *by them.*
D.	তাহারে, *to him.*	তাহার্দিগেরে, *to them.*

	Singular	Plural
A.	তাহাতে, তাহাহইতে, *from him.*	তাহার্দিগেতে, তাহার্দের হইতে, তাহার্দিগ্হইতে, *from them.*
P.	তাহার, *his.*	তাহার্দের, তাহার্দিগের, *their.*
L.	তাহায়, *in him.*	তাহার্দিগেতে, *in them.*

The other forms differ nothing from the above, except in leaving out the middle হ্া. *Exam.* Ac. তাকে, Inst. তাতে, &c.

17. The neuter pronoun সে and তাহা, also যে and যাহা, are the same in all the cases except the nominative singular.

সে, তা, তাহা, *it, that.*

Neuter.

Singular and Plural.

N. সে, তা, তাহা, *it,* or *they.*
Ac. তাহা, তা, *it* or *them.*
I. তাহাতে, তাতে, *by it* or *by them.*
D. তাহাতে, তাতে, *to it* or *them.*
A. তাহাতে, তাহাহইতে, তাতে, তাহইতে, *from it* or *from them.*
P. তাহার, তার, *its* or *their.*
L. তাহায়, তাহাতে, তায়, তাতে, *in it* or *in them.*

18. কাহ্া and কা are substituted for কি, *what?* in the oblique cases. স্ is optionally inserted before the terminations in all the cases except the accusative. The substitution does not take place when স্ is inserted.

19. The termination হইতে of the ablative case is never used when স্ is inserted.

Neuter.

Singular and Plural.

N. কি, *what?*
Ac. কাহা, or কা, *what?*
I. কাহাতে, কাতে, কিসে, কিসেতে, *by what?*
D. কাহাতে, কাতে, কিসে, কিসেতে, *to what?*
A. কাহাতে, কাতে, কাহাহইতে, কাহইতে, কিসে, কিসেতে, *from what?*
P. কাহার, কার, কিসের, *what's?*
L. কাহায়, কায়, কাহাতে, কাতে, কিসে, কিসেতে, *in what.*

20. The pronominal adjectives are কোন্, *what?* কোন, *any*, কিছু, *any, some*, অন্য, *another*. The two first are indeclinable. The two last are regularly declined without any substitution.

21. যেং, যেকেহ, *whosoever, whatsoever*, are declined as the simple forms, but in the last member only.

22. কোন কেহ, *any one*, is declined in the last member only.

SECTION VI.

Of Verbs, (ক্রিয়ার পদ.)

1. The Bengalee verbs, with a few exceptions, are formed from the S*u*ngskr*i*t*a* dhat*oo*s or roots.

2. There is but one conjugation of Bengalee verbs.

3. Verbs are conjugated in two forms, one agreeing with the honorific pronouns, the other with those of inferiority or contempt. There is no difference in the terminations of the singular and plural verb.

4. There are two voices, the active (কর্ত্তৃবাচ্য), and the passive (কর্ম্মবাচ্য).

5. There are three modes, the Indicative, (স্বার্থ;) the Subjunctive, (আশংসার্থ;) and the Imperative, (অনুমত্যর্থ).

6. The indicative mode has eight tenses (কাল), of which two are present (বর্ত্তমান), viz. the first aorist (নিত্য প্রবৃত্ত বর্ত্তমান), and the present definite (শুদ্ধ বর্ত্তমান); five are past (অতীত or ভূত), viz. the second aorist (অপরোক্ষ ভূত); the perfect, (অদ্যতন ভূত;) the imperfect definite, (শুদ্ধ ভূত,) the perfect, (অদ্যতনানদ্যতন ভূত;) the pluperfect, (অনদ্যতন ভূত;) and one is future, (ভবিষ্যৎ.) Four of these, viz. the first and second aorist, the imperfect, and the future, are formed immediately from the root. The

others are formed by means of the neuter or auxiliary verb.

7. অর্ is substituted for the final ঋ of a verbal root when it is followed by a termination. *Exam.* করে, *he does,* ধরে, *he holds,* মরে, *he dies,* from the roots কৃ, ধৃ, and মৃ.

8. The final ঋ of জাগৃ, *to awake,* is rejected when followed by a verbal termination. *Exam.* জাগে, *he wakes.*

9. Dhat*oo*s with a penultimate nasal, following অ, usually soften it down to ঁ when followed by the verbal terminations. The vowel অ is made long. *Exam.* আঁকি, *I mark,* বাঁটে, *he shares out,* বাঁধে, *he binds,* from the roots অঙ্ক or অক্—ই, বণ্ট, and বন্ধ.

10. জান্ is substituted for জ্ঞা, *to know ;* দি, for দা, *to give ;* পি, for পা, *to drink ;* মাপ্, for মা, *to measure ;* in a few instances তিষ্ঠ, but generally থাক্, for স্থা *to be situated ;* উড়, for ডী, *to fly,* when preceded by the preposition উৎ ; ল, for নী, *to take ;* শু, for শী, *to lie down ;* শুন্, for শ্রু, *to hear ;* হো, for ভূ, *to be ;* গিল্ for গৃ, *to swallow ;* কিন্, for ক্রী, *to buy ;* and বিক্, or বেচ্, for ক্রী, when preceded by the preposition বি, meaning *to sell ;* গায়্, for গৈ, *to sing,* and দেখ্, for দৃশ্, *to see,* when they are conjugated.

11. খ্ is optionally substituted for the final ক্ষ of a verbal root when it is conjugated. *Exam.* রাখে, রক্ষে, *he keeps,* শিখে or শিক্ষে, *he learns.*

12. গি is substituted for যা, *to go,* in the perfect and pluperfect tense, and গে in the imperfect tense. *Exam.* গেলাম, *I went,* গিয়াছে, *he has gone,* গিয়াছিল, *he had gone.*

13. ধু is substituted for ধাব্, when it means *to wash*, and দৌড়্, when it signifies *to run*. *Exam.* ধুইলাম, *I washed* ; দৌড়িলাম, *I run.*

14. আছ্ is substituted for অস্, *to be.* This root is only used in the first aorist and the imperfect tense. In the imperfect tense, the আ of the substituted আছ্ is optionally omitted. *Exam.* সে আছে, *he is,* ছিলাম or আছিলাম, *I was.*

15. আই is substituted in the first aorist for য়া, *to go,* when it is preceded by the preposition আ. আস্ is substituted for it in all the other tenses. In the imperfect tense both forms are used. Compounded with this preposition, the verb means *to come.* *Ex.* আইসি, *I come,* আইলাম, or আসিলাম, *I came,* আসিয়াছি, *I have come.*

16. কহ্ is substituted for কথ্, *to speak.* *Exam.* প্রভু কহিতেছেন, *the master speaks.*

17. The ই of লিখ্, *to write,* is optionally changed to এ. *Exam.* লিখি or লেখি, *I write.*

18. The ই of the দি, which is substituted for দা, *to give,* is changed to এ, in the second and third persons of the first aorist, and in the imperative mode. *Exam.* দেও, *thou givest,* দেয় or দেন্, *he gives,* দেও, *give.*

19. ও is substituted for the final উ of a dhat*oo* or its substitute, in the second and third persons of the first aorist, and in the imperative mode. *Exam.* ধো, *wash* or *thou washest* ; ধোয়, or ধোন্, *he washes* ; ধোউক্, ধোউন্, *let him wash.*

20. পা is substituted for আপ্, *to obtain,* when it is preceded by the preposition প্র. *Exam.* আমি পাই, *I obtain,* পাইলাম, *I obtained.*

21. দাঁড় is substituted for দণ্ড, *a staff,* which is then conjugated as a verb, and signifies *to stand;* আ is inserted before the terminations of all the tenses. *Exam.* সে দাঁড়ায়, *he stands;* সে দাঁড়াইল, *he stood;* দাঁড়াও, *stand.*

22. খা is substituted for খাদ্, *to eat.* *Exam.* খাইলাম, *I ate;* খাই, *I eat;* খাও, *eat.*

23. The first person honorific of the first aorist is formed by affixing ই, the second by affixing ও, and the third by এন; the first person inferior by affixing ই, the second by ইস্, and the third by এ.

24. The second aorist is formed by affixing ইতাম্, ইতা, ইতেন্, respectively, for the three persons honorific, and ইতাম্, ইতিস্, ইত, for the inferior.

25. The imperfect indefinite is formed by affixing ইলাম্, ইলা, ইলেন্, respectively for the three persons honorific; and ইলাম্, or ইনুঁ, for the first, ইলি for the second, and ইল, or ইলেক্, for the third person inferior.

26. The future honorific is formed by affixing ইব, or ইম, for the first, ইবা, for the second, and ইবেন, for the third person; the inferior by ইব, or ইম, for the first person, ইবি, for the second, and ইবে, or ইবেক্, for the third.

Of Participles.

27. The present participle active is usually made by

affixing ত, to the root or its substitute. *Exam.* করত, *doing,* লিখত, *writing.*

28. When this participle agrees with a word in the nominative case, it is formed by ত, as above, and when with a word in the accusative case, or compounded with the neuter verb, it is formed by ইতে. *Exam.* কহত, *speaking;* তাহারদিগকে আসিতে দেখিয়া তিনি কহিলেন, *seeing them coming he said.*

29. ও is usually inserted after a vowel before the ত of the participle. *Exam.* দেওত, *giving;* পাওত, *obtaining.*

30. The present participle of those roots which are conjugated in Sungskrita, only in the middle voice, is formed by affixing আন, or মান, to the root. *Exam.* বর্দ্ধমান, *increasing;* শয়ান, *reposing.*

31. The present participle passive is made by affixing মান to the root; য় is usually inserted before this termination. *Exam.* নীয়মান, *in the state of being taken away;* ক্রিয়মাণ, *in the state of being done.*

32. The adverbial participle is formed by affixing ইয়া, to the verbal root. This participle is sometimes contracted by omitting the initial ই of the termination, and except the root or its substitute have a final হ or র, sometimes by omitting the final, য়া. Some, but improperly, substitute এ for the termination ইয়া. This participle is either present or past as suits the meaning of the sentence. *Exam.* কহিয়া, কহি, কহে, *speaking,* or *having spoken;* করিয়া, করি, করে, *doing,* or *having done;* ফেলিয়া, ফেলি, ফেল্যা, or ফেলে, *having thrown.*

33. A participle used to connect sentences which have different agents is formed by affixing হইলে, to the root. This form agrees with the absolute case of the Greek and Latin languages. *Exam.* তাহা করিলে আমি যাইব, *when he has done that I will go.*

34. The passive participle past is usually formed by affixing ত to the root. *Exam.* কৃত, *done;* ধৃত, *seized;* খ্যাত, *renowned.*

35. In all instances where a dhat*oo* has not an *unubun*dh*a* উ, ই is inserted before the termination of the passive participle. This is also the case in the causal. *Exam.* পতিত, *fallen;* বর্দ্ধিত, *increased;* গমিত, *made to go.*

36. The final ম্ of a dhat*oo* is changed to ন্, before the ত of the passive participle, unless ই is inserted. In this case, the penultimate অ is made long. *Exam.* দান্ত, *suppressed;* বান্ত, *vomited;* শ্রান্ত, *wearied.*

37. In many instances a final ন্ or ম্ is omitted before the ত of the passive participle. *Exam.* হত, *smitten;* গত, *gone.*

38. The final হ্ of a dhat*oo* is often changed to গ, in which case the ত of the passive participle is changed to ধ, and sometimes it coalesces with it, and both together are expressed by ঢ়. Frequently both forms are employed. *Exam.* মূঢ়, or মুগ্ধ from মুহ্, *to lose sensation.*

39. In some instances ন is substituted for the ত of the passive participle. *Exam.* ক্ষীণ, *decayed, emaciated,* পূর্ণ, *filled.*

40. ঈর্ is substituted for the ৠ of a verbal root to form the passive participle. Whenever this is the case, ন is employed instead of the affix ত. *Exam.* বিকীর্ণ, *scattered;* বিস্তীর্ণ, *spread out;* অবতীর্ণ, *descended, incarnate.*

41. The passive participle of a great proportion of the S*u*ngskr*i*t*a* roots is employed in this language, even though their use in a verbal form be not admitted. These participles are exactly the same as in the S*u*ngskr*i*t*a*, even if they are anomalous in that language. *Exam.* পক্ক, *ripened;* ক্ষুব্ধ, *agitated;* সোঢ়, *borne.*

42. The verbal noun in আ is often used for the passive participle. *Exam.* লেখা, *written.*

43. The gerund is formed by affixing ইতে to the root or its substitute. This form has been usually, though improperly, called the Infinitive mode. *Exam.* দেখিতে, *to see,* or *for the purpose of seeing.*

44. Another gerund, or more properly a verbal noun, is formed by affixing ইবা to the root. This word is regularly declined. *Exam.* করিবা, *a doing;* করিবাতে, *by doing;* করিবার, *of doing.*

45. From the present participle in ইতে, and the adverbial participle in ইয়া, constructed with the auxiliary verb, four tenses are formed, viz. the present definite, the imperfect definite, the perfect, and the pluperfect.

46. The present definite is formed by conjugating the present participle in ইতে, with the present tense of the auxiliary, its first letter আ being lost in the S*u*ndh*i* or

joining. *Exam.* করিতেছি, *I am doing,* contracted from করিতে আছি.

47. The imperfect definite is made by conjugating one form of the imperfect tense of the auxiliary with the present participle in ইতে. *Exam.* করিতেছিলাম, *I was doing.*

48. The perfect tense is formed by conjugating the adverbial participle in ইয়া with the present tense of the auxiliary. *Exam.* করিয়াছি, *I have done.*

49. The pluperfect is formed by conjugating the adverbial participle in ইয়া with one form of the imperfect tense of the auxiliary. *Exam.* করিয়াছিলাম.

50. From these observations the following scheme of the verbal termination (বিভক্তি) is formed:

INDICATIVE MODE.

FIRST AORIST.

	Honorific.	Inferior.
1.	ই.	ই.
2.	অ, ও.	ইস্.
3.	এন্.	এ.

SECOND AORIST.

1.	ইতাম্.	ইতাম্.
2.	ইতা.	ইতিস্, ইতি.
3.	ইতেন্.	ইত.

IMPERFECT.

1.	ইলাম্, ইনুঁ.	ইলাম্, ইনুঁ.
2.	ইলা.	ইলি.
3.	ইলেন্.	ইল, ইলেক্.

FUTURE TENSE.

1.	ইব, ইমু.	ইব, ইমু.
2.	ইবা.	ইবি.
3.	ইবেন্.	ইবে, ইবেক্.

IMPERATIVE MODE.

1.	ই.	ই.
2.	অ, ইও.	—, ইস্.
3.	উন্.	উক্.

SUBJUNCTIVE MODE.

PRESENT TENSE.

1.	ই.	ই.
2.	অ, ও.	ইস্.
3.	এন্, ন্.	এ.

PRETER TENSE.

1.	ইতাম্.	ইতাম্.
2.	ইতা.	ইতিস্, ইতি.
3.	ইতেন্.	ইত.

FUTURE TENSE.

1.	ইব, ইমু.	ইব, ইমু.
2.	ইবা.	ইবি.
3.	ইবেন্.	ইবে, ইবেক্.

PARTICIPLES.

Present, ত, ইতে. *Adverbial*, ইয়া, য়া, ই, এ.

Passive, ত, ন. *Gerund*, ইতে, ইবা.

N. B. The initial ই of the terminations is often suppressed after a vowel.

The Auxiliary Verb আছি, *I am.*

INDICATIVE MODE.

PRESENT TENSE.

	Honorific.	Inferior.
1.	আমি আছি, *I am.*	মুই আছি, *I am.*
2.	তুমি আছ, *thou art.*	তুই আছিস্, *thou art.*
3.	তিনি আছেন, *he is.*	সে আছে, *he is.*

IMPERFECT.

Honorific.

1. আমি আছিলাম্, ছিলাম্ or ছিনুঁ, *I was.*
2. তুমি আছিলা or ছিলা, *thou wast.*
3. তিনি আছিলেন্ or ছিলেন্, *he was.*

Inferior.

1. মুই আছিলাম্, ছিলাম্ or ছিনুঁ, *I was.*
2. তুই আছিলি or ছিলি, *thou wast.*
3. সে আছিল or ছিল, *he was.*

কৃ, *to do, to make, to perform,* is thus conjugated:

INDICATIVE MODE.

FIRST AORIST.

	Honorific.	Inferior.
1.	আমি করি *I do.*	মুই করি, *I do.*
2.	তুমি কর, *thou dost.*	তুই করিস্, *thou dost.*
3.	তিনি করেন্, *he does.*	সে করে, *he does.*

PRESENT DEFINITE.

Honorific.	Inferior.
1. আমি করিতেছি, *I am doing.*	মুই করিতেছি, *I am doing.*
2. তুমি করিতেছ, *thou art doing.*	তুই করিতেছিস্, *thou art doing.*
3. তিনি করিতেছেন, *he is doing.*	সে করিতেছে, *he is doing.*

51. The terminations of the present definite are frequently contracted to ইচ্ছি, ইচ্ছ, ইচ্ছেন্, ইচ্ছি, ইচ্ছিস্, ইচ্ছে. *Exam.* আমি করিচ্ছি, *I am doing.*

SECOND AORIST.

Honorific.	Inferior.
1. আমি করিতাম, *I did.*	মুই করিতাম্, *I did.*
2. তুমি করিতা, *thou didst.*	তুই করিতিস্, *thou didst.*
3. তিনি করিতেন্, *he did.*	সে করিত, *he did.*

IMPERFECT.

Honorific.	Inferior.
1. আমি করিলাম্ or করিনুঁ, *I did.*	মুই করিলাম্ or করিনুঁ, *I did.*
2. তুমি করিলা, *thou didst.*	তুই করিলি, *thou didst.*
3. তিনি করিলেন্, *he did.*	সে করিল or করিলেক্, *he did.*

IMPERFECT DEFINITE.

Honorific.

1. আমি করিতেছিলাম্ or করিতেছিনুঁ, *I was doing.*
2. তুমি করিতেছিলা, *thou wast doing.*
3. তিনি করিতেছিলেন্, *he was doing.*

Inferior.

1. মুই করিতেছিলাম্ or করিতেছিনুঁ, *I was doing.*
2. তুই করিতেছিলি, *thou wast doing.*
3. সে করিতেছিল, *he was doing.*

PERFECT.

Honorific.

1. আমি করিয়াছি, *I have done.*
2. তুমি করিয়াছ, *thou hast done.*
3. তিনি করিয়াছেন্, *he has done.*

Inferior.

1. মুই করিয়াছি, *I have done.*
2. তুই করিয়াছিস্, *thou hast done.*
3. সে করিয়াছে, *he has done.*

PLUPERFECT.

Honorific.

1. আমি করিয়াছিলাম্ or করিয়াছিনুঁ, *I had done.*
2. তুমি করিয়াছিলা, *thou hadst done.*
3. তিনি করিয়াছিলেন্, *he had done.*

Inferior.

1. মুই করিয়াছিলাম or করিয়াছিনুঁ, *I had done.*
2. তুই করিয়াছিলি, *thou hadst done.*
3. সে করিয়াছিল, *he had done.*

FUTURE.

Honorific.

1. আমি করিব or করিমুঁ, *I will* or *shall do.*
2. তুমি করিবা, *thou wilt* or *shalt do.*
3. তিনি করিবেন্, *he will* or *shall do.*

Inferior.

1. মুই করিব or করিমুঁ, *I will* or *shall do.*
2. তুই করিবি, *thou wilt* or *shalt do.*
3. সে করিবে or করিবেক্, *he will* or *shall do.*

IMPERATIVE MODE.

Honorific.

1. করি, *I will do.*
2. করহ্, কর, করিও, *do thou* or *do ye.*
3. করুন, *may he* or *they do.*

Inferior.

1. করি, *we will do.*
2. কর্, করিস্, *do thou* or *do ye.*
3. করুক্, *may he* or *they do.*

52. The first person imperative is used when any action is proposed to be done. *Exam.* আমরা যাই, *we (will) go.*

53. Sometimes the address is made by the verb আইস, *come,* in the second person. *Exam.* আইস আমরা যাই, *come, we will go.*

SUBJUNCTIVE MODE.

54. The subjunctive mode is formed by constructing the first and second aorist, or the future tense, of the indicative mode, with the subjunctive particle যদি, *if,* or যে, *that.*

PRESENT TENSE.

Honorific.

1. যে আমি করি, *that I may do.*
2. যে তুমি কর, *that thou mayest do.*
3. যে তিনি করেন, *that he may do.*

Inferior.

1. যে মুই করি, *that I may do.*
2. যে তুই করিস্, *that thou mayest do.*
3. যে সে করে, *that he may do.*

PRETER TENSE.

Honorific.

1. যদি আমি করিতাম্, *if I had done.*
2. যদি তুমি করিতা, *if thou hadst done.*
3. যদি তিনি করিতেন্, *if he had done.*

Inferior.

1. যদি মুই করিতাম্, *if I had done.*
2. যদি তুই করিতিস্ or করিতি, *if thou hadst done.*
3. যদি সে করিত, *if he had done.*

FUTURE TENSE.

Honorific.

1. যদি আমি করিব, *if I shall do.*
2. যদি তুমি করিবা, *if thou shalt do.*
3. যদি তিনি করিবেন্, *if he shall do.*

Inferior.

1. যদি মুই করিব, *if I shall do.*
2. যদি তুই করিবি, *if thou shalt do.*
3. যদি সে করিবে, *if he shall do.*

PARTICIPLES.

Present, করিতে and করত, *doing*.
Continuative, করিতে২, *doing, continuing to do.*
Adverbial, করিয়া, করি, কর্য্যা, করে, করিলে.
Passive, কৃত, *done*.

GERUNDS.

করিতে, *for the purpose of doing.*
করিবা, *doing.* করিবার, *of doing.* করিবারে, *in doing.*

Of Compound Verbs.

55. Most of the verbs may, in some of their forms, be compounded with other verbs, and when thus compounded, acquire a meaning different from what they had in their simple state.

The verb স্থা, *to stand, to be situated, to remain*, compounded with the adverbial participle, gives the verb a subjunctive or conditional sense if constructed with a subjunctive particle. If there be no particle constructed therewith, it conveys an idea of the action being customary, or probable. থাক্ is substituted for the root স্থা, *to stand. Exam.* আমি করিয়া থাকি, *I do it usually.*

Example.

FIRST AORIST.

1. যদি আমি করিয়া থাকি, *if I may do.*
2. যদি তুমি করিয়া থাক, *if thou mayest do.*
3. যদি তিনি করিয়া থাকেন্, *if he may do.*

It may be conjugated in this manner through all the tenses.

56. The adverbial participle is frequently compounded with the verb ফেল, *to throw.* This compound verb conveys the idea of the action's being done completely, or in an excessive degree.

Example.

1. আমি করিয়া ফেলি, *I do (it) effectually.*
2. তুমি করিয়া ফেল, *thou dost (it) effectually.*
3. তিনি করিয়া ফেলেন্, *he does (it) effectually.*

Thus through all the tenses.

Neuter verbs, and some others do not admit of this compound form.

The verb লগ্, *to come in contact,* is frequently compounded with the gerund in ইতে. The verb thus compounded, gives the idea of the commencement of the action. The vowel of লগ্ is made long when it is conjugated.

Example.

FIRST AORIST.

1. আমি করিতে লাগি, *I begin to do.*
2. তুমি করিতে লাগ, *thou beginnest to do.*
3. তিনি করিতে লাগেন্, *he begins to do.*

Thus through all the tenses.

57. A form which may be called the potential mode is formed by compounding the verb পার্, *to be able*, with the gerund in ইতে.

Example.

FIRST AORIST.

1. আমি করিতে পারি, *I can do.*
2. তুমি করিতে পার, *thou canst do.*
3. তিনি করিতে পারেন্, *he can do.*

Thus through all the tenses.

চা, *to desire*, is often compounded with the gerund in ইতে, and gives the idea of wishing or desiring to perform the action.

Example.

FIRST AORIST.

1. আমি করিতে চাই, *I desire to do.*
2. তুমি করিতে চাও, *thou desirest to do.*
3. তিনি করিতে চান, *he desireth to do.*

Thus through all the tenses.

পা *to obtain*, (substituted for the root আপ when preceded by the preposition প্র,) is frequently constructed with the gerund in ইতে, and the verb thus compounded has the meaning of obtaining the privilege of doing the action, or of suffering the thing intended by the verb. *Exam.* সে দেখিতে পাইল, *he saw.*

যা, *to go*, is constructed with the adverbial participle of all neuter verbs, and usually gives the idea of becoming what the verb indicates or of coming into the state which it describes. *Exam.* সে হইয়া গিয়াছে, *it is become.* সে উঠিয়া যায়, *he ariseth.*

OF CAUSAL VERBS.

58. Causal verbs (প্রেরণার্থ) are formed from the simple verbs (স্বার্থ) by inserting আ between the original root and the verbal termination. Verbs with a final আ require the insertion of ব before the characteristic আ of the causal, which must be pronounced like the English *w.* *Exam.* খাবাই, *I cause him to eat.*

N. B. It is very common to insert য় instead of ব. This is, however, improper, and, to mark its impropriety more decidedly, it is constantly pronounced like *w.*

The final of দা, *to give,* is changed to এ; before the causal increment, ব must be inserted. *Exam.* দেবাইল, *he caused to give.* Dhatoos with a final উ change it to ও; before the causal increment, ব must be inserted. *Exam.* ধোবাইলাম, *I caused to wash.*

করা, *to cause to do.*

INDICATIVE MODE.

FIRST AORIST.

Honorific.

1. আমি করাই, *I cause to do.*
2. তুমি করাও, *thou causest to do.*
3. তিনি করান্, *he causeth to do.*

Inferior.

1. মুই করাই, *I cause to do.*
2. তুই করাইস, *thou causest to do.*
3. সে করায়, *he causeth to do.*

PRESENT DEFINITE.

Honorific.

1. আমি করাইতেছি, *I am causing to do.*
2. তুমি করাইতেছ, *thou art causing to do.*
3. তিনি করাইতেছেন, *he is causing to do.*

Inferior.

1. মুই করাইতেছি, *I am causing to do.*
2. তুই করাইতেছিস, *thou art causing to do.*
3. সে করাইতেছে, *he is causing to do.*

SECOND AORIST.

Honorific.

1. আমি করাইতাম, *I caused to do.*
2. তুমি করাইতা, *thou causedst to do.*
3. তিনি করাইতেন, *he caused to do.*

Inferior.

1. মুই করাইতাম্, *I caused to do.*
2. তুই করাইতিস্ or করাইতি, *thou causedst to do.*
3. সে করাইত, *he caused to do.*

IMPERFECT.

Honorific.

1. আমি করাইলাম্ or করাইনুঁ, *I caused to do.*
2. তুমি করাইলা, *thou causedst to do.*
3. তিনি করাইলেন্, *he caused to do.*

Inferior.

1. মুই করাইলাম্ or করাইনুঁ, *I caused to do.*
2. তুই করাইলি, *thou causedst to do.*
3. সে করাইল or করাইলেক্, *he caused to do.*

IMPERFECT DEFINITE.

Honorific.

1. আমি করাইতেছিলাম্ or করাইতেছিনুঁ, *I was causing to do.*
2. তুমি করাইতেছিলা, *thou wast causing to do.*
3. তিনি করাইতেছিলেন্, *he was causing to do.*

Inferior.

1. মুই করাইতেছিলাম্ or করাইতেছিনুঁ, *I was causing to do.*
2. তুই করাইতেছিলি, *thou wast causing to do.*
3. সে করাইতেছিল, *he was causing to do.*

PERFECT.

Honorific.

1. আমি করাইয়াছি, *I have caused to do.*
2. তুমি করাইয়াছ, *thou hast caused to do.*
3. তিনি করাইয়াছেন্, *he hath caused to do.*

Inferior.

1. মুই করাইয়াছি, *I have caused to do.*
2. তুই করাইয়াছিস, *thou hast caused to do.*
3. সে করাইয়াছে, *he hath caused to do.*

PLUPERFECT.

Honorific.

1. আমি করাইয়াছিলাম্ or করাইয়াছিনুঁ, *I had caused to do.*
2. তুমি করাইয়াছিলা, *thou hadst caused to do.*
3. তিনি করাইয়াছিলেন, *he had caused to do.*

Inferior.

1. মুই করাইয়াছিলাম or করাইয়াছিনুঁ, *I had caused to do.*
2. তুই করাইয়াছিলি, *thou hadst caused to do.*
3. সে করাইয়াছিল, *he had caused to do.*

FUTURE.

Honorific.

1. আমি করাইব, করাব, or করাম, *I will cause to do.*
2. তুমি করাইবা, or করাবা, *thou wilt cause to do.*
3. তিনি করাইবেন্ or করাবেন্, *he will cause to do.*

Inferior.

1. মুই করাইব, করাব or করামু, *I will cause to do.*
2. তুই করাইবি or করাবি, *thou wilt cause to do.*
3. সে করাইবে or করাবে, *he will cause to do.*

IMPERATIVE MODE.

Honorific.

1. করাই, *I will cause to do.*
2. করাও, *cause to do.*
3. করাউন্, *let him* or *them cause to do.*

Inferior.

1. করাই, *I will cause to do.*
2. করাও, *cause to do.*
3. করাউক্, *let him* or *them cause to do.*

SUBJUNCTIVE MODE.

PRESENT.

Honorific.

1. যে আমি করাই, *that I may cause to do.*
2. যে তুমি করাও, *that thou mayest cause to do.*
3. যে তিনি করান্, *that he may cause to do.*

The inferior form is like the first aorist indicative.

PRETER.

Honorific.

1. যদি আমি করাইতাম্, *if I had caused to do.*
2. যদি তুমি করাইতা, *if thou hadst caused to do.*
3. যদি তিনি করাইতেন্, *if he had caused to do.*

The inferior is like the second aorist indicative.

FUTURE.

Honorific.

1. যদি আমি করাইব, *if I shall cause to do.*
2. যদি তুমি করাইবা, *if thou shall cause to do.*
3. যদি তিনি করাইবেন্, *if he shall cause to do.*

The inferior is like the future indicative.

The compound verbs are used in the causal the same as in the simple verb, though more sparingly. A single example of one tense will be sufficient to shew the manner of forming them.

FIRST AORIST.

Honorific.

1. যদি আমি করাইয়া থাকি, *if I may cause to do.*
2. যদি তুমি করাইয়া থাক, *if thou mayest cause to do.*
3. যদি তিনি করাইয়া থাকেন্, *if he may cause to do.*

This mode is regularly conjugated through the same tenses as the indicative.

PARTICIPLES.

Present, wanting.

Continuative, করাইতে২, *causing to do.*

Adverbial, করাই, করাইয়া, করাইলে, *causing*, or *having caused to do.*

59. The passive participles of causal verbs are generally formed by affixing ন to the causal root. The Sungskrita form is also used. *Exam.* করান, *caused to be done.* কারিত, *caused to be done.*

GERUNDS.

করাইতে, *to cause to do.* করাইবা, *causing to do.* *Gen.* করাইবার, *of causing to do.* *Loc.* করাইবারে, *in causing to do.*

60. Intransitive verbs when they become transitive must be in the causal. *Exam.* শস্য শুকে, *the corn dries.* সূর্য্য শস্যকে শুকায়, *the sun dries the corn.* সে পুড়ে, *it burns.* অগ্নি তাহাকে পোড়ায়, *the fire burns him.*

61. That form of the verb which expresses the necessity of the act is formed by constructing the third person of ভূ, *to be*, with the gerund in ইতে. হ্ is substituted for ভূ, *to be.* The verb in this form is governed by the accusative case.

Examples.

PRESENT.

Honorific.

1. আমাকে যাইতে হয়, *it is necessary for me to go.*
2. তোমাকে যাইতে হয়, *it is necessary for thee to go.*
3. তাহাকে যাইতে হয়, *it is necessary for him to go.*

PRETER.

Honorific.

1. আমাকে যাইতে হইল, *it was necessary for me to go.*
2. তোমাকে যাইতে হইল, *it was necessary for thee to go.*
3. তাহাকে যাইতে হইল, *it was necessary for him to go.*

FUTURE.

Honorific.

1. আমাকে যাইতে হবে, *I must go.*
2. তোমাকে যাইতে হবে, *thou must go.*
3. তাহাকে যাইতে হবে, *he must go.*

The pluperfect tense is sometimes used.

The form of the inferior is like that of the honorific. The pronoun only is changed.

OF THE NEGATIVE VERB.

FIRST AORIST.

Honorific.

1. আমি করি না, *I do not.*
2. তুমি কর না, *thou dost not.*
3. তিনি করেন্ না, *he doth not.*

The present definite, second aorist, and future are formed like the above by putting the participle না after the simple verb.

62. The preter tenses are the same as the present, except that the negative particle নাই is substituted for না.

PRETER.

Honorific.

1. আমি করি নাই, *I did not,* or *have* or *had not done.*
2. তুমি কর নাই, *thou didst not,* or *hast* or *hadst not done.*
3. তিনি করেন্ নাই, *he did not,* or *hath* or *had not done.*

Inferior.

1. মুই করি নাই, *I did not,* or *have* or *had not done.*
2. তুই করিস্ নাই, *thou didst not,* or *hast* or *hadst not done.*
3. সে করে নাই, *he did not,* or *hath* or *had not done.*

63. Sometime the particle না is put after the simple forms of the imperfect and pluperfect.

64. It is common to express the present tense of the neuter verb ভূ, *to be,* in its negative form, by inflicting the particle as if it were a verb.

Examples.

Honorific.

1. আমি নয়ি or নহি, *I (am) not.*
2. তুমি নও or নহ, *thou (art) not.*
3. তিনি নন্ or নহেন্, *he (is) not.*

Inferior.

1. মুই নয়ি or নহি, *I (am) not.*
2. তুই নয়িস্ or নহিস্ *thou (art) not.*
3. সে নয় or নহে, *he (is) not.*

নার is sometimes substituted for the verb পার্ *to be able,* when preceded by the negative particle না, and is regularly conjugated as a verb. *Exam.* আমি নারিলাম্, *I could not;* তুমি নার, *thou canst not.*

65. In poetry, the imperfect tense of those verbs which have a final র় or ল is often contracted. *Exam.* করিলাম্ is contracted to কৈলাম্; বলিলাম্ to বৈলাম্; মরিলাম্ to মৈলাম্.

66. The word বট, *indeed,* is inflected like a verb, in the first aorist, and agrees with the agent of the verb to which it belongs. *Exam.* বটি, বট, বটেন্, and (infer.) বটে.

OF THE PASSIVE VOICE.

67. The passive voice is made two ways: the first by conjugating the verb যা, *to go,* with the verbal noun in আ; the other by conjugating the verb ভূ, *to be,* with the passive participle. হ is substituted for ভূ, *to be.*

Examples.

FIRST AORIST.

1. আমি করা যাই or কৃত হই, *I am done.*
2. তুমি করা যাও or কৃত হও, *thou art done.*
3. তিনি করা যান্ or কৃত হন্, *he or it is done.*

Thus through all the modes and tenses.

Remarks on the Verbs.

68. The first aorist is used when we express an action proper to the agent without any particular designation of the time. *Ex.* পক্ষিরা উড়ে, *birds fly,* পণ্ডিতেরা বিচার করে, *wise men investigate,* i. e. flying is the common action of birds, and wise men employ themselves in investigating things. This does not mean that birds are *now* in the act of flying, or that wise men are *now* investigating.

69. When a person accedes to, or makes a proposal, his assent or proposal is expressed in the first person of the imperative mode. *Exam.* Question. তুমি কি বাটী যাইবা, *will you go home?* Answer. আমি যাই, *I will go.* আমরা বাটী যাই, *let us go home.*

70. The present definite is used to denote that the agent is at that instant employed in the act. *Exam.* আমি বিচার করিতেছি, *I am (now) investigating.*

71. The second aorist expresses an action which the agent was accustomed to do, or usually did, some time ago. *Exam.* বালককালে আমি পাঠশালায় বিদ্যাভ্যাস করিতাম্, *in my childhood I studied the sciences at school, viz. I was accustomed, or used to do so.* এক আসনে নব রাত্রি আসন করিত বহু প্রকারে সাধন ভজন করিত, *he sat (viz. used to sit) for nine nights on one seat, and performed (viz. used to perform) many kinds of ceremonies and acts of worship.*

72. The imperfect tense expresses an action as past. The time when it was done is usually, though not always,

expressed. *Exam.* আমি কল্য বাটী আইলাম্, *I came home yesterday.*

73. The perfect tense expresses an action as compleated. *Exam.* আমি তাহাকে সে কথা কহিয়াছি, *I have told him that affair.*

74. The pluperfect is frequently used instead of the imperfect. In general it indicates, that the action was done prior to some other circumstance expressed or understood. *Exam.* তিনি তাহারদের বড় দুঃখ করিয়াছিলেন্, *he gave* or *had given them great trouble.*

75. The future tense expresses the time to come. *Exam.* ভাদ্র মাসে বৃষ্টি হবে, *there will be rain in the month* Bhadra.

76. In the respectful style, the form of the future is often used for the imperative. *Exam.* মহাশয় সহসা এমত করিবেন না, *don't act hastily in this manner, Sir.* আপনি এ মূর্খ চাকরের কথায় আস্থা করিবেন্ না, *don't, Sir, confide in what this ignorant servant says.*

77. The form of the first aorist is sometimes used for the imperative. *Exam.* মহাশয় তাহাকে এক লিখন আমার তরে লিখেন্, *be pleased, Sir, to write a letter to him on my account.*

78. The simple form of the subjunctive mode is made by constructing the first and second aorist, and the future tense of the indicative, with a subjunctive particle. The supposition and inference are usually, though not always, to be expressed in the same tense. *Exam.* তুমি যদি সে কথা আমাকে কহিতা তবে আমি কার্য্য সিদ্ধি করিতাম্, *if thou*

hadst spoken to me about that affair, I should have accomplished it. যদি সে জন অকৃতজ্ঞ হয় তবে আমি তাহার আর উপকার করিব না, *if that man be ungrateful, I will give him no more assistance.*

79. A sentence expressing the reason or scope of a preceding sentence, is expressed by the particle যে, *that,* governing a verb in the subjunctive mode, present tense. *Exam.* এ কথিত আছে যে তোমরা প্রত্যয় কর, *this was spoken that ye might believe.*

80. The compound form of the subjunctive is often used without a particle of supposition or inference. This, in the future tense, expresses the probability of the action's being done; in the present tense, it indicates that the action is customary. *Exam.* সে যাইয়া থাকিবে, *he may go, (hereafter).* সে জন আসিয়া থাকে, *he is accustomed to come.*

81. The present participle in ত is used when it describes some circumstance respecting the agent of a verb, and that in ইতে when it describes some circumstance respecting the object. *Exam.* পণ্ডিত মনে২ বিচার করত কথা কহিলেন, *the philosopher, reflecting, spake.* এক জন অন্ধ ভিক্ষা করত পথের ধারে বসিত, *a blind man used to sit begging by the way-side.* বংশ না হইতে তুমি যাইতে চাহ ছাড়িয়া, *you want to leave (me) without offspring.* তাহাকে আসিতে দেখিলাম, *I saw him coming.*

82. The adjective in ঈ is often used as a present participle. *Exam.* আমি তোমার পশ্চাদ্গামিকে পরামর্শ দিলাম, *I gave advice to (him who is) following you.*

83. The continuative participle, though expressing the

present time, denotes a continuance of the action till its end be accomplished, or till some other event occur. *Exam.* যাইতে২ উত্তরিল, *continuing to go, he arrived.* খাইতেং তৃপ্ত হইলাম্, *continuing to eat, or by eating, I am satisfied.*

84. The adverbial participle in ইয়া is used to connect several sentences governed by the same agent, and upon which some other action depends. *Exam.* রাজা পণ্ডিতের পূর্ব্বোপকার স্মরণ করিয়া মন্ত্রিরদের বাক্য আদর না করিয়া পণ্ডিতকে ছাড়িয়া দিতে আজ্ঞা করিলেন, *the prince, remembering the former assistance of the philosopher, and not regarding the words of the counsellors, ordered him to be set at liberty.*

85. If an action depend upon several preceding actions, done by different agents, the participle in ইলে is used before a new agent is introduced. This participle usually agrees with the absolute case of the Latin language. *Exam.* সলিমন বিস্তর শওগাত দিয়া আক্বরের সহিত সাক্ষাৎ করিলে বাদশাহ্ তাঁহার নিবেদন শুনিলেন্ পরে তাহার অনুগ্রহেতে অনুগৃহীত হইয়া তিনি পদার্পিত হওনের ফরমান ও বিচিত্র খেলাত পাওনেতে কৃতার্থ হইয়া গৌড়ে বাহুড়িলেন, *When Solyman, by means of presents, had obtained an interview with Akbur, the king attended to his request; after which, being indulged with his favour, and raised to dignity by obtaining an order of appointment to office, and a variegated robe, he returned to Gowr.*

86. When it is asserted that some end will be accomplished, or some event happen, if a given circumstance take place, the supposition is frequently expressed by the participle in ইলে, instead of the verb in the subjunctive mode. *Exam.* বৃষ্টি হইলে ধান্য হইবে, *if there be rain, there will be rice.*

87. The verbal noun in আ has frequently the power of a passive participle. *Exam.* ধর্ম্ম পুস্তকে লেখা আছে, *it is written in the Bible.*

88. The gerund, when constructed with কারণ, জন্য, তরে, নিমিত্ত or হেতু, appears to have nearly the same use as the verbal noun when constructed with the same words. *Exam.* সে কার্য্য করণের কারণ, করার কারণ, or করিবার কারণ তিনি আইলেন, *he came for the purpose of doing that business.*

89. The gerund in the genitive case has often the nature of an adjective. *Exam.* ধান্য রুপিবার কাল, *the season of planting rice.* বুনিবার কাল, *sowing time.*

90. There are three ways of expressing the passive voice. In the first, the form of the verb is the same as in the active voice, but the agent is in the instrumental case, and the subject in the nominative. *Exam.* বাঘে or বাঘেতে মানুষ খাইয়াছে, *a man was devoured by a tyger.* In the second the verbal noun in আ is constructed with যা, *to go. Exam.* তাহারদের নাম মাত্র শুনা যায়, *merely their names are heard of;* and in the third verb ভূ, *to be,* is constructed with the passive participle. *Exam.* তাহারা আনুপুর্ব্বিক না জাননেতে ক্ষোভিত হয়, *they are distressed at not knowing all the circumstances in order.*

91. The vocative particles are often placed after the verb in the imperative mode. *See the examples, page* 19.

92. দিকি, দিখি, দিনি and সিনি, are put after verbs in the imperative mode, to arrest the attention of the person addressed. *Exam.* দেখদিকি কেমন ফল, *see, what fruit !*

93. কো is often added to the first aorist of verbs immediately after the negative particle, when the preter is designed to be expressed. When this particle is thus used, নি is usually substituted for the negative নাই. *Exam.* আমি করি নি কো, *I have not done it.* আমি কখন করি নি কো, *I never did it.*

94. তো, when prefixed or added to a verb in the present tense, frequently implies a supposition that some effect will follow. *Exam.* আমিতো যাই, or আমি যাইতো, *I will go (then it will probably be done.)*

95. তো prefixed or affixed, as above, often indicates a resolution to perform an action though success may be uncertain. *Exam.* আমিতো করিব (হবে বা না হবে), *I will do it (but the result is uncertain).* এমন মেঘতো করিয়াছে (বৃষ্টি হবে বা না হবে), *there are so many clouds, (shall we have rain or not?)*

96. তো before a negative sometimes marks a certainty respecting the agent, but implies an uncertainty respecting others. *Exam.* আমিতো করি নাই, *I did not do it, (I cannot say what another may have done.)* আমি লোকতো দেখি নাই, *I see no one; (I suppose I must do it myself.)* আমিতো করি নাই আর কেহ করিয়া থাকে কি,—*I did not do it, some other person may have done it, or—(you may have done it yourself.)*

SECTION VII.

OF THE FORMATION OF WORDS.

1. A very large proportion of the words in the Bengalee language are formed from the S*u*ngskr*i*t*a* roots, with which, and the manner of forming words from them, every student of the Bengalee, and other languages derived from that source, ought to be well acquainted.

2. Words are, 1. Verbals, or such as are formed immediately from verbal roots.

2. Derivatives, or words formed from verbals by the addition of certain terminations or formative syllables.

3. Compound words, or such as arise from compounding two or more simple words.

3. It would scarcely come within the limits of a grammar intended for common use, to insert rules for the formation of every word used in the language. The increments employed in forming verbals, except those which only apply to single words, or to words not introduced into the Bengalee language, follow:

অন, and আ, affixed to the root, form nouns substantive which convey the idea of the performing of the action. As there is no infinitive mode to the verb in any of the Indian languages, these substantives are constructed with another word in the genitive case to perform the office of that mode in other languages. *Exam.* লেখন or লেখা,

the writing; দর্শন and দেখা, *the seeing of a thing*; তাহার দর্শন অতিসুখদায়ক, *to see him is very pleasant.*

তি, affixed to the root, forms a class of substantives which have the same meaning as English words which terminate in -ion, -ness, &c. In some instances নি is substituted for তি. *Exam.* কৃতি, *an action*; ভক্তি, *devotedness*; মতি, *opinion, mind*; বুদ্ধি, *intellect*; হানি, *loss.*

থক is affixed to a few roots to form nouns of agency. *Exam.* গাথক, *a singer.*

A very large class of words, chiefly nouns of agency, is made by affixing তৃ to the root. In the Bengalee language আ is substituted for the ঋ of this affix, unless the word form the first member of a compound word. *Exam.* বক্তা, *a speaker*; জ্ঞাতা, *one who knows.*

A considerable number of nouns substantive, denoting the thing which the verb performs, are made by affixing ন to the root. *Exam.* যত্ন, *an endeavour*; স্বপ্ন, *a dream.*

Nouns of agency are formed by affixing অক to verbal roots. In most instances the vowel of the root is increased by vriddhi when অক is affixed. These words, though generally employed as substantives, are in reality adjectives. *Exam.* কারক, *an agent*; লেখক, *a writer*; ধাবক, *a runner.*

The affixing of অ to a root produces a considerable number of substantive nouns. When this অ is affixed, ক is substituted for the final চ of the dhatoo, and গ for a final জ. *Exam.* কর, *a hand*; বহ, *a carrier*; ব্যতিরেক, *an exception*; ত্যাগ, *relinquishment.*

Nouns of instrumentality are formed by several affixes; the principal are ত্র, অস্, উস্, ইস্ and মন্: of these, those formed by ত্র occur more frequently than the others. *Exam.* নেত্র, *the eye*, or *organ of sight*; দংষ্ট্র *a tooth*; যোত্র, *a cord to fasten an ox to the yoke*; রজস্, *dust*, or *that which stains*; চক্ষুস্, *the eye*; সর্পিস্, *ghee*; জন্মন্, *birth.* The finals of the three last words, and of others similarly formed, are usually omitted in the Bengalee language.

Many substantives are formed by the affix য্. These, being feminine in S*u*ngskr*ita*, must receive the feminine increment আ. *Exam.* ক্রিয়া, *a work*; শয্যা, *a bed*; বিদ্যা, *science.*

A class of substantives, also feminines in S*u*ngskr*ita*, is formed by the affix অ. These must receive the feminine increment আ. *Exam.* দিদৃক্ষা, *a desire to see*; জিজ্ঞাসা, *a question*; viz. *a wish to know*; তুলা, *a balance*; ইচ্ছা, *the will*; জরা, *old age*; তারা, *a star*; ধারা, *a rivulet, a way, a course* or *custom*; চিন্তা, *anxiety*; পূজা, *worship.*

উ, affixed to verbal roots, gives rise to a great number of words. *Exam.* বায়ু, *the wind*; স্বাদু, *taste* or *relish*; জানু, *a thing.*

A considerable number of words is formed by the affix তু. *Exam.* সেতু, *a bridge*; ধাতু, *a metallic ore*; জন্তু, *an animal*; বস্তু, *a thing*; হেতু, *a cause.*

The affixing of ম gives rise to a good number of substantives. The vowel of the root to which this increment is affixed must be changed by goon. *Exam.* হোম, *a burnt-sacrifice*, সোম, *the moon*, ক্ষেম, *happiness.*

Sometimes, however, the vowel of the dhat*oo* is not changed by goon. *Exam.* ধূম, *smoke ;* হিম, *cold ;* রুক্ম, *gold.*

The affixing of র gives rise to a great number of words. *Exam.* চন্দ্র, *the moon ;* উদ্র, *an otter ;* সূর, *the sun ;* গৃধ্র, *a vulture ;* ছিদ্র, *a hole.*

4. Those who wish to become better acquainted with the etymology of Bengalee words, will do well to study carefully the chapter of কৃদন্ত and উনাদি affixes in the S*u*ngskr*ita* grammar. The rules here given will, however, suffice for the formation of most of the substantive verbals, which are used in the language.

OF THE FORMATION OF VERBAL ADJECTIVES.

5. All the participles above-mentioned, page 36, except the present participle in অত or ইতি, the adverbial, the conditional, and the repeated one, are often used as adjectives. *Exam.* বর্দ্ধমান, *increasing ;* কৃত, *done.*

6. Adjectives which indicate a tendency or bias to some particular action are formed by affixing ইষ্ণু, ষ্ণু, স্নু, নু, উক, আলু, রু, মর, উর, ঊক, বর, র, উ, and a few other affixes of less frequent occurrence. The above increments cannot be affixed to any root at pleasure, but are proper to certain roots pointed out by S*u*ngskr*ita* grammarians. *Exam.* বর্দ্ধিষ্ণু, *increasing ;* জিষ্ণু, *conquering ;* স্থাস্নু, *stationary ;* ধৃষ্ণু, *daring ;* ঘাতুক, *murderous ;* শয়ালু, *disposed to sleep ;* দারু, *sharp ;* অদ্মর, *ravenous ;* ভঙ্গুর, *brittle ;* বিদুর, *wise ;* বাবদূক, *garrulous ;* ভাস্বর, *splendid ;* নশ্বর, *perishable ;* হিংস্র, *hurtful ;* নম্র, *humble ;* লিপ্সু, *covetous ;* জিজ্ঞাসু, *inquisitive.*

7. A large class of very useful adjectives, indicating a bias to the act, or simply engagedness therein, is formed by affixing ইন্ to the root. The vowel of the root must be increased by vriddhi. In the Bengalee language the final ন্ is rejected, and the ই preceding it is made long. This is, however, in the nominative case alone. *Exam.* স্থায়ী, *continuing;* কারী, *performing;* অপরাধী, *guilty;* অহঙ্কারী, *proud.*

8. Adjectives may be formed to almost any extent by compounding a verbal root with some other word. These roots receive the affix অ after them. In some instances the vowel of the root is increased by goon, and in other by vriddhi.

9. When the roots কৃ, *to do,* and সৃ, *to move,* compounded with words as above, require the vowel to be increased by vriddhi, the words, though adjectives, are commonly used as substantives in the Bengalee language. *Exam.* কুম্ভকার, *a potter;* viz. *pitcher-making.*

10. More frequently, however, these two roots are thus employed when the vowel only suffers the alteration occasioned by goon. Words thus formed are adjectives, though some of them are employed as substantives. *Exam.* পুরঃসর, *preceding;* তুষ্টিকর, *pleasing;* যশস্কর, *fame-producing.* But ভাস্কর, *irradiating,* viz. *the sun;* চিত্রকর, *a painter;* নিশাকর, *night-making;* viz. *the moon;* and some others, are usually accounted substantives.

11. The roots হন্, *to kill;* চর্, *to move;* গৈ, *to sing;* ধৃ, *to hold;* কৃ, *to do;* সৃ, *to move;* গম্, *to go;* জ্ঞা, *to know;* স্থা, *to be situated;* দা, *to give;* and জন্, *to be produced;* are

compounded with nouns to form adjectives which respectively indicate, *destroying, moving, singing, holding, doing, moving, knowing, situated in, giving*, or *produced from*, that indicated by the word to which they are joined. By the above, and some other rules, the above roots respectively make the syllables ঘ্ন, চর, গ, ধর, কর, গ, জ্ঞ, স্থ, দ, and জ. *Exam.* ধনঘ্ন, *wealth-destroying* ; জলচর, *aquatic* ; সামগ, *chanting the Sama-veda* ; দণ্ডধর, *swaying the sceptre*, viz. *a king* ; শান্তিকর, *tranquillizing* ; ভয়ঙ্কর, *terrific* ; অগ্রসর, *preceding* ; নীচগ, *descending* ; সর্ব্বত্রগ, *going every where* ; সর্ব্বজ্ঞ, *omniscient* ; গৃহস্থ, *situated in the house* ; আনন্দদ, *giving pleasure* ; শ্রমজ, *arising from labour.*

Those roots which are distinguished in the general list by the *unubundha* ডু, are by the affix ত্রিম formed into adjectives which indicate a quality arising from the act. *Exam.* কৃত্রিম, *artificial.*

Adjectives corresponding with those which in English end in -able, or -ible, are formed by affixing তব্য, অনীয়, or য, to the root. These words are properly indefinite participles passive, indicating that the act is to be performed, or ought, or is worthy, or is fit or proper, to be performed. *Exam.* কর্ত্তব্য, *practicable, proper to be done* ; দানীয়, *proper to be given* ; দৃশ্য, *visible, fit to be seen.*

The final of the roots ending in আ, is usually changed to এ, when য is affixed. *Exam.* দেয়, *proper to be given*, জ্ঞেয়, *capable of being known.*

Of Derivative Words, (তদ্ধিত.)

By affixing certain syllables or letters to verbals, or to compounds, or even to other derivative words, a numerous class of derivative words is formed.

Of Patronymics.

These words are mostly adjectives in the Bengalee language, but as the custom of neglecting the substantive with which they should be constructed has prevailed, they are often used as the substantives themselves.

Many patronymics are made by affixing ই to words with a final অ, and increasing the first vowel of the word by vriddhi. *Exam.* কার্ষ্ণি, *a descendant of Krishna.*

এয় is affixed to feminines ending in আ, ই or ঈ, to make patronymics. A final ঈ is rejected before this affix. The first vowel of the word must be made long by vriddhi. *Exam.* গৌরেয়, *a descendant of* গৌরী.

A considerable number of patronymics is formed by affixing য, and others are made by অয়ন. The first vowel must be lengthened by vriddhi. *Exam.* গার্গ্য, *a descendant of the sage Gurga.* আশ্বায়ন, *the descendant of a horse.* নড়ায়ন, *a descendant of the sage Nura.*

Some patronymics are formed by affixing অ. The first vowel is lengthened by the rules of vriddhi. *Exam.* শৈব, *a Levite ;* বাশিষ্ঠ, *a descendant of Vushishtha.*

There are a few other affixes which are employed in the formation of patronymics, but as the words formed by them are few, and seldom used, it is unnecessary to add them here.

Of Gentile Nouns.

Gentile nouns, or such as denominate a people from their country, city, or town, are formed by the same affixes, and in the same manner as patronymics, and like them are in reality adjectives. *Exam.* গৌড়ীয়, *inhabiting Gowr;* দেশী or দেশীয়, *inhabiting a country;* বঙ্গীয়, *inhabiting Bunga* or *Bengal;* also বাঙ্গালা, *Bengalee.*

Gentiles may also be made at pleasure by affixing দেশী, দেশ্য or দেশীয়, to the name of the country. *Exam.* চীনদেশী, চীনদেশ্য or চীনদেশীয়, also চীনী, *a Chinese.*

Of Collectives.

Collectives are formed in Sungskrita by a great number of affixes, and those words are copiously admitted into the Bengalee language. The most usual methods of forming collectives are by the affixing of অ, and increasing the first vowel of the word by vriddhi, or by the affixing of য্য, or তা. *Exam.* লৌক, *a multitude of people;* মানব, *a multitude of men;* বন্যা, *a flood;* জনতা, *a multitude of men.*

Of Abstract Substantives.

These may be formed from all adjectives, and from a very great number of substantives, by affixing to the word ত্ব or তা. *Exam.* ভদ্রতা or ভদ্রত্ব, *goodness;* ঈশ্বরতা or ঈশ্বরত্ব, *lordship;* প্রভুত্ব or প্রভুতা, *lordship, domination, sovereignty;* দেবতা, *deity.*

Abstract substantives may be also generally formed by affixing অ or য, and increasing the first vowel of the word by vriddhi. *Exam.* গৌরব, গুরুতা or গুরুত্ব, *greatness;* মার্দব, মৃদুতা or মৃদুত্ব, *mildness;* স্থৈর্য্য, স্থিরতা or স্থিরত্ব, *stedfastness;* সৌন্দর্য্য, সুন্দরতা or সুন্দরত্ব, *beauty.*

Abstract nouns are formed from names of colours, and

some other words, by affixing ইমন্. The final ন্ is rejected in the Bengalee language, and the vowel of ম is made long. These may also be formed by the two preceding rules. *Exam.* রক্তিমা, রক্ততা or রক্তত্ব, *redness ;* শুক্লিমা, শুক্লত্ব, শু-ক্লতা or শৌক্ল, *whiteness ;* গরিমা, গুরুত্ব, গুরুতা or গৌরব, *greatness, importance.*

Of Derivative Adjectives.

These are very numerous, and may be formed by different affixes, so as to express almost every possible shade of meaning. The most general affixes are অ, য, and ইক, with the first vowel lengthened by *vriddhi.*

By the above three affixes, adjectives of colour are formed from words meaning colouring substances. *Exam.* হারিদ্র, *coloured with turmeric ;* লাক্ষিক, *dyed with lac.*

Adjectives denominating food from the vessel or instrument with which it is cooked, sects from their leader or god, and a country from its productions or inhabitants, are formed by these three affixes. *Exam.* শূল্য, *roasted ;* শৈব, *worshipping Shiva ;* ঔডুম্বর, *abounding with fig trees.*

Adjectives indicating the mere existence of some quality or property, are formed by the affixing of য় or ইক. *Exam.* বাঙ্গ, *Bengalee ;* আধ্যাত্মিক, *existing in the subject ;* পারলৌকিক, *belonging to a future state ;* ঐহিক, *belonging to the present world.*

Many adjectives of this class are made by affixing য্. *Exam.* আদ্য, *first, principal ;* দন্ত্য, *dental ;* ওষ্ঠ্য, *labial.*

Adjectives of this kind are formed from compounds which have বর্গ, *a class,* for their last member, by affixing ঈয়, য়, or ইন্.* If the first member of the compound be a letter of the alphabet, ঈয় only is affixed. *Exam.* কবর্গীয়, *belonging to the first class of consonants* ; অর্জুনবর্গীয়, অর্জুনবর্গ্য, or অর্জুনবর্গী, *belonging to Urjoona's party.*

Adjectives which indicate that a thing is composed or made of a particular substance or material are formed by affixing অ to the name of the material, and making the first vowel of the word long by vriddh*i*. *Exam.* পালাশ, *made of Pulasha wood ;* (Butea frondosa.)

Many adjectives of this kind are made by affixing ময়. *Exam.* কাষ্ঠময়, *wooden ;* যবময়, *barley ;* লোহময় or লৌহ, *iron.*

A very large class of adjectives expressive of the existence of the thing from which they are formed is made by affixing বৎ or মৎ. In the masculine these are changed to বান্ and মান্, and in the feminine to বতী and মতী. *Exam.* বলবৎ, neut. বলবান্, masc. বলবতী, fem. *strong ;* শ্রীমৎ, neut. শ্রীমান্, masc. শ্রীমতী, fem. *glorious.*

Those words which have a final or penultimate ম, অ, or আ, or a final consonant, except it be a nasal, a semi-vowel, or a sibilant, require the affix বৎ, and nearly all others require মৎ. *Exam.* লক্ষ্মীবান্, *fortunate ;* জ্ঞানবান্, *wise ;* বুদ্ধিমান্, *intelligent.*

* The final of this affix and all others ending in ইন্, is rejected in the Bengalee language, and the ই made long in the nominative case.

The affix বিন্ is affixed to words with a final অস্, and a few other words. *Exam.* তেজস্বী, *resplendent,* মায়াবী, *illusive.*

In the Sungskrita language many other affixes are used to form adjectives of this class, and words thus formed are often used in the Bengalee language: those of most frequent occurrence are ইল, শ, র, ইন, ইক, আলু, শালিন্, and উল. *Exam.* পিচ্ছিল, *slippery;* লোমশ, *hairy;* মধুর, *sweet;* মলিন, *filthy;* মায়িক, *delusive;* দয়ালু, *compassionate;* ধৈর্য্যশালী, *patient;* বাতুল, *hypochondriac.*

ইন্ is affixed to all compounds of which the last member is অর্থ, *an object;* শীল, *a disposition;* ধর্ম্ম, *religion;* or বর্ণ, *a sort;* and to a very large number of other words, to form this kind of adjectives. *Exam.* জলার্থী, *desirous of water;* সুশীলী, *good-natured;* ব্রাহ্মণধর্ম্মী, *of the brahminical religion;* রক্তবর্ণী, *red;* ধনী, *rich;* জ্ঞানী, *wise;* দুঃখী, *afflicted.*

SECTION VIII.

Of Compound Words, (সমাস.)

Compound words are formed by joining a number of simple words to each other. The last member only can be inflected. There are six classes of compound words.

1. The first class called দ্বন্দ্ব consists of those compounds which are formed by collecting several substantives into one word. This is usually done by omitting the copulative conjunction. *Exam.* হে মহারাজ সকল ঋতুরাজ বসন্ত আপনকার বিলাস বিপিনসমূহে প্রবেশ করিলেন বনরাজি নবীন পল্লব ফল পুষ্পস্তবক মঞ্জরী ভারেতে পরম শোভাবিষ্ট হইয়াছেন, *O great prince, Spring, the king of all the seasons, has entered into all your pleasure-grounds, and is ornamented with a load of* FOREST-ADORNING NEW SHOOTS, FRUITS, FLOWERS, CLUSTERS, and FLOWER-SPIKES. N. B. The words put in small capitals answer to the compound.

2. The second class, called বহুব্রীহি, consists of compound epithets formed by joining two or more words together. This class is very extensive, and may be formed at the pleasure of the speaker. *Exam.* মৃগাক্ষী, *deer-eyed;* শশিমুখী, *moon-faced;* গৌরাঙ্গ, *white-bodied;* পীতাম্বর, *clothed in yellow;* দিগম্বর, *clothed with the points of the compass,* viz. *naked;* বাঘাম্বর, *clothed with a tyger's skin;* দুরাত্মা, *evil-minded, wicked.*

3. The third class is called কর্ম্মধারয়, viz. compound words formed by the construction of a substantive with its

adjective. *Exam.* মাতা ক্ষুদ্র বালকের বিষয়ে অতি চিন্তান্বিতা আছেন, *the mother is very anxious for her little child.*

N. B. This rule explains the reason why adjectives are not inflected when the substantive is expressed; the adjective being supposed to drop its inflection, and to form a compound word with the substantive. This is also the case with several of the pronouns. *Exam.* এ সকল লোকেরদিগকে, *to all these people,* not, *all these to the people.*

4. A substantive frequently becomes the adjective to another substantive; in which case its inflection is not expressed. *Exam.* সাহেব লোকেরা, *gentlemen;* মুহরিগিরি, *the employment of a writer.*

The words আপনকার বিলাস বিপিনসমূহে, *in all your pleasure-grounds,* see (example to Rule 1) are an example of this compound. If the words had not formed a compound, it must have been rendered *your pleasure-ground in the collection;* because the last word only being inflected, the foregoing words would in that case be separated from it, and stand in the nominative case.

5. মহা is substituted for মহৎ, *great,* when compounded with a substantive. *Exam.* মহারাজ, *a great king;* মহাবল, *great strength.*

The final of রাজন্, *a king,* and অহন্, *a day,* is omitted when either of them is the last member of a compound. *Exam.* মহারাজ, *a great king;* পরমাহ, *a fine day.*

অহন্, *a day;* preceded by সর্ব্ব, *all;* by words which denote a particular part of time, by numerals, or indeclinables, is changed to অহ্ন. *Exam.* সর্ব্বাহ্ন, *the whole day;* মধ্যাহ্ন, *mid-day;* পুর্ব্বাহ্ন, *the forenoon.*

6. The fourth class, called তৎপুরুষ, consists of words formed by compounding a substantive in any case, with a verb, omitting the inflection of the noun. The compound words thus formed are adjectives. *Exam.* বনরাজী, *forest-adorning,* see (the example to Rule 1). In this example the noun is in the accusative. জলপুর্ণ, *full of water;* সোনামড়া, *overlaid with gold;* and হস্তকৃত, *made by hands;* are instances of participles compounded with a noun in the third case. The inflection of the fourth case is omitted in দেবদায়ী, *giving to the gods.* The inflection of the fifth case is omitted in বৃক্ষপতিত, *fallen from a tree;* and গৃহাগত, *come from the house.*

7. When one substantive is constructed with another in the sixth case, the two words may form a compound of this class, by omitting the inflection of the case. The compounds thus formed are often substantives. *Exam.* সুখাকাঙ্খা, *the desire of happiness;* কার্য্যাধ্যক্ষ, *the superintendent of the work;* গৃহকর্ত্তা, *the master of the house.*

Words derived from the Sungskrita, when they are compounded, revert back to the original form which they had in that language before they were declined. *Exam.* পিতৃধর্ম্ম, *the religion of a father;* মাতৃস্নেহ, *a mother's affection;* তৎপরে, *after that;* তদুপরে, *upon that.* These words cannot be written পিতা ধর্ম্ম, মাতা ধর্ম্ম, সে পরে or সে উপরে, which they must have been if they had been formed from the Bengalee nominative.

8. মৎ and আমা are substituted for আমি, *I;* ত্বৎ and

তোমা, for তুমি, *thou;* অস্মৎ for আমরা, *we;* যুষ্মৎ, for তোমরা, *ye;* তৎ, for তিনি, তিঁহ, and সে, *he;* যৎ, for যিনি, and যে, *who;* এতৎ, for ইনি, and এ, *this;* and কিং, for কে, *who?* and কেহ, *any one;* when they are compounded with other words. *Exam.* আমাদবের কারণ, *for us all;* মদ্দশা, *my condition;* মদ্দ্বারা, *through me;* তোমাবিপরীতে, *in opposition to you;* ত্বদ্বাক্য, *your words;* অস্মদ্ভাষা, *our language;* যুষ্মদ্দেশ, *your country;* তন্নিমিত্তে, *on that account;* যজ্জন্যে, *on which account;* কিম্বদন্তী, *some person speaking.*

9. A passive participle is often the first member of these compounds. *Exam.* হতবুদ্ধি, *bereft of understanding;* হীনবুদ্ধি, *of destitute of understanding;* হৃষ্টচিত্ত, *glad-hearted;* জাতক্রোধ, *of excited anger;* হৃতসর্ব্বস্ব, *stripped of his all.*

10. The following words, viz. কারী, কারক, *doing;* গামী, *going;* দায়ী, দায়ক, *giving;* বাদী, *speaking;* হারী, *taking away;* এষী, *desirous;* ইচ্ছু, or ইচ্ছুক, *desirous;* অন্বেষী, *seeking;* রাজী, *adorning;* নাশী, নাশক, *destroying;* জনক, *producing;* অনুযায়ী, *following upon;* স্থায়ী *standing;* বর্ত্তী, *existing;* ভাবী, *existing, future;* জ্ঞাপক, *making known;* সূচক, *indicating;* স্থাপক, *placing, fixing;* উপকারী, উপকারক, *assisting;* অপেক্ষী, অপেক্ষক, *expecting, wanting;* ভাষী, *speaking;* ত্যাগী, *abandoning;* ক্রয়ী *buying;* বিক্রয়ী, *selling;* দর্শী, দর্শক, *seeing;* ধারী, ধারক, *assuming, wearing;* আকাঙ্ক্ষী, *desirous;* and, if required, any other verbal formed by the affixes অক, and ঈ (ইন্) may be employed as the last member of a compound of the fourth class. *Exam.* প্রেমকারী, প্রেমকারক, *loving;* পথগামী, *going in the road;* সুখদায়ী, সুখদায়ক, *giving happiness;* বাক্যবাদী, *speaking words;* পাপহারী, *taking away crime;* হিতৈষী, হিতেচ্ছুক, *benevolent;* সুখান্বেষী, *seeking happiness;* দেশরাজী, *country-adorning;* পাপনাশী, পাপনাশক, *crime-*

destroying; সুখজনক, *happiness-producing;* আজ্ঞানুযায়ী, *according to the command;* চিরস্থায়ী, *long-continuing;* গ্রামবর্ত্তী, *in the village;* তদ্ভাবী, *being that;* কার্য্যজ্ঞাপক, *giving information of the business;* অনিষ্টসূচক, *indicating evil;* দ্রব্যস্থাপক, *placing the thing;* মিত্রোপকারী, মিত্রোপকারক, *friend-assisting;* মিত্রাপেক্ষী, মিত্রাপেক্ষক, *friend-expecting;* পরুষভাষী, *speaking abusively;* ধর্ম্মত্যাগী, *apostatizing;* ধান্যক্রয়ী, *purchasing rice;* শস্যবিক্রয়ী, *selling corn;* দীর্ঘদর্শী, দীর্ঘদর্শক, *long-sighted, provident;* অস্ত্রধারী, *bearing arms;* জগদ্ধারক, *supporting the world;* সুখাকাঙ্ক্ষী, *desirous of happiness.*

Passive participles are compounded with other words to any desired extent. The following, viz. স্থিত, *situated;* গত, *gone;* কৃত, *done;* দত্ত, *given;* উক্ত, *spoken;* জ্ঞাত, *known;* গ্রস্ত, *involved in;* ত্যক্ত, *abandoned;* প্রাপ্ত, *obtained;* হত, *smitten;* যুক্ত, যুত, *united to;* অন্বিত, *connected with;* অভীষ্ট, *desired;* আবিষ্ট, *engaged in;* যোগ্য, *capable;* বিশিষ্ট, *affected by;* রহিত, হীন, and বিহীন, *destitute of;* are the most common. These participles made the last member of the compound word. *Exam.* হস্তস্থিত, *situated in the hand;* হস্তগত, *gone into or held in the hand;* হস্তকৃত, *made by the hand;* দেবদত্ত, *given by a god;* বেদোক্ত, *mentioned in the veda;* সমাচার জ্ঞাত, *acquainted with the news;* আপদ্গ্রস্ত, *involved in calamity;* ঈশ্বরত্যক্ত, *forsaken by God;* ধনপ্রাপ্ত, *possessed of wealth;* দৈবহত, *smitten by Providence;* আনন্দযুক্ত, আনন্দযুত, আনন্দান্বিত, *joyful;* পাপাভীষ্ট, *devoted to sin;* পাপাবিষ্ট, *engaged in crime;* সম্মানযোগ্য, *worthy of honour;* আহ্লাদবিশিষ্ট, *joyful;* ধর্ম্মহীন, ধর্ম্মবিহীন, ধর্ম্মরহিত, *destitute of religion.*

11. Words in the seventh case are compounded as follows: *Exam.* হরিভক্তি, *faith in Hurri;* বঙ্গবাসী, *an inhabitant of Bengal;* viz. *one dwelling in Bengal;* শিখরবাসী, *a*

mountaineer or *one dwelling on a mountain* ; জলচর, *living in the water, aquatic* ; খেচর, *moving in the air* ; ভূচর, *moving on the ground.*

12. The fifth class (দ্বিগু) consists of compound words formed by collecting several things together by means of a numeral. *Exam.* ত্রিভুবন, *the three worlds.* চতুর্দ্দিগ, *the four cardinal points.* চতুর্যুগ, *the four yoogs.*

13. The sixth class is called অব্যয়ীভাব. It consists of compounds, the first member of which is a preposition, an adverb, or some other indeclinable word. These compounds are usually adverbs. *Exam.* যাবজ্জীবন, *as long as life lasts.* যথাশক্তি, *to the utmost extent of one's power.*

14. Many words which signify the mutual act of two or more persons, are formed by doubling the simple words. The first member of these words must terminate in আ, and the last in ই. *Exam.* হানাহানি, *a mutual wounding,* from হানি, *a wounding;* গালাগালি, *mutual abuse ;* from গাল, *a cheek ;* মারামারি, *a battle,* or *mutual smiting, from* মারা, *a smiting ;* পিটাপিটী or তাড়াতাড়ি, *a promiscuous pursuit ;* from পিটা and তাড়া, *a pursuing, a smiting.*

The words ভূত, *become,* and কৃত, *done ;* are often compounded with another word to signify the becoming or being made the thing expressed by that other word ; ঈ is in this case inserted before these two participles. *Exam.* বশীভূত, *become subject to ;* যাথার্থিকীকৃত, *justified ;* পবিত্রীকৃত, *sanctified.* The two following words are compounded without the insertion of ঈ. বহির্ভূত, *on the outside ;* বহিষ্কৃত, *excluded.*

15. In this language a word is often followed by a sound of no meaning which rhymes with it. These two words produce a compound which means the thing expressed by the principal word, together with all others of the same class. *Exam.* জলটল কিছু আছে ? *is there any water* or *other liquid ?* বাসনকুসন সব লইয়া গিয়াছে, *he has taken away all the plates, dishes, and other vessels.*

SECTION IX.

OF INDECLINABLE PARTICLES.

Under this head are included Adverbs, Prepositions, Conjunctions, and Interjections.

Of Adverbs.

1. Adverbs are naturally indeclinable, but many of those words which correspond with adverbs in other languages are, in this, nouns substantive, which are generally put in the locative case to express the circumstances of verbs. They always govern the possessive case of the noun with which they are constructed. *Exam.* তিনি রাজার নিকটে আইলেন, *he came near*, or, *to the prince.*

2. Nouns substantive, and adjectives, are often constructed with the participles করিয়া or হইয়া, or with the words রূপ or পূর্ব্বক, to express the circumstances of verbs. *Exam.* তিনি যত্ন করিয়া or যত্নপূর্ব্বক সে কর্ম্ম করিলেন, *he did that business carefully.* বিলক্ষণরূপে করিয়াছ, *you have done excellently.*

3. Adverbs are usually divided into those of Time, Place, and Circumstance. Some of the most common follow:

Time.

যখন, *when.*	পশ্চাৎ, পাছে, *after.*
তখন, *then.*	কদাচ, *at any time.*
এখন, *now.*	কোনকালে, *at any time.*
কখন, *when ?*	উত্তরে, পরে, তৎপরে, তারপর, *afterwards.*
যবে, *when.*	ভোরে, প্রত্যূষে, *early in the morning.*

তবে, *then.*

পুনর্ব্বার, পুনরায়, পুনরপি, আরবার, *again.*

এবে, *now.*

পরশ্ব, *the day before yesterday, the day after to-morrow.*

কবে, *when?*

তরশ্ব, *two days ago, two days hence.*

বৈকালে, সায়ংকালে, *in the evening.*

নিত্য, *constantly.*

প্রভাতে, সকালে, *in the morning.*

সদাকাল, সর্ব্বক্ষণে, *always.*

যাবৎ, *whilst.*

সদা, সদৎ, সর্ব্বদা, *always.*

তাবৎ, *so long.*

পূর্ব্বে, আগে, *before.*

কল্য, কালি, *yesterday, to-morrow.*

তৎকালে, *at that time.*

অদ্য, আজি, *to-day.*

Place.

এখানে, *here.*

ওথায়, *there (in sight.)*

ওখানে, *there (in sight.)*

সেথায়, *there.*

সেখানে, *there.*

মধ্যে, *in the midst.*

যেখানে, *where.*

মাঝে, *in the midst.*

কোথা, *where?*

নিকটে, *near.*

কোথায়, *where?*

দূরে, *far off.*

যথায়, *where.*

সম্মুখে, *before, opposite to.*

তথায়, *there.*

সাক্ষাৎ, *in the presence.*

এথায়, *here.*

আশপাশ, *on all sides.*

Miscellaneous.

যে, *that.*

কিছু, *a little.*

মন্দ, *slowly.*

কেমন, *how?*

নাই, না, নয়, নে, *not.*

যেমন, *as.*

প্রায়, *almost.*

তেমন, *so.*

অনুসারে, *according to.*

এমন, *thus.*

ক্রমে২, *by little and little.*
বিস্তর, *much, very.*
যত, *how many.*
কত, *how many?*
এত, *so many.*
কেন, *why?*
হেন, *so.*
তেন, *in that manner.*
বটে, *truly, indeed.*
ভাল, *well.*
তত, *as many.*
অতি, *very.*
অনুক্রমে, *successively.*
দৈবে, *by divine interposition.*
পরষ্পর, *mutually.*
পরম্পরা, *from one to another.*
নিরর্থ, *to no purpose.*
বৃথা, or ব্যর্থ, *in vain.*

4. খান, স্থান, স্থল and ঠাঁই, compounded with the pronouns এ, *this;* ও, *that;* কোন্, *what?* যে, *what;* and, কোন, *any;* form adverbs of place. ক্ষণ, *an instant;* or মত, *a manner;* compounded with the above pronouns form adverbs of time, or circumstance. These words must be in the locative case. *Exam.* আমি সেখানে গিয়াছি, *I went thither;* সে স্থানে তিনি দাঁড়াইলেন, *he stood there.*

5. ই, *indeed, even,* is frequently added to nouns, pronouns, verbs, and other particles to make the word emphatic. *Exam.* জলেই, *even in the water.* আমিই, *I indeed.* আমি তাহাই করি, *I do it indeed.* কিছুই নয়, *nothing truly.*

6. বা, *or, and,* is added in the same manner to signify doubt. *Exam.* সে তাহা করিবে বা না করিবে, *will he do it or not?*

Of Prepositions.

7. Many nouns substantive, and adjectives are in the Bengalee language constructed with other nouns or pronouns to perform the office of prepositions, viz. তল, *the bottom.* সহিত, সঙ্গ, সহ, সাতে, *society, with.* তুল্য, সমান, *equal.* উপরে, *upon.* দিগ্ or দিক্, *a point of the compass.*

নীচ, *low.* হেতু, কারণ, নিমিত্ত, *a cause ;* জন্য, *arising from ;* and several other words. These are generally in the locative case, and follow a noun or pronoun which is in the possessive. This has induced some to call them post-positions. *Exam.* মেজের উপরে, *on the table.* মেজের নীচে, *beneath the table.*

8. Some adjectives, which form compounds with those nouns or pronouns with which they are constructed, are employed for the same purpose, as কর্ত্তৃক, করণক, পূর্ব্বক, পর্য্যন্ত, and a few more. *Exam.* তোমাকর্ত্তৃক, *by thy agency.* তোমাকরণক, *by thy instrumentality.* তোমার অনুগ্রহপূর্ব্বক, *by* or *through thy favour.* তোমার আইসনপর্য্যন্ত, *till your coming.*

9. The following twenty inseparable prepositions are compounded with nouns or verbs, and cause a variation from their simple meaning :—

প্র generally conveys the idea of excellence or eminence. *Exam.* প্রকাশ, *display.* প্রদক্ষিণ, *a going to the south.*

পরা conveys the idea of the action's being reflected, or of its having an opposite direction to what it would have in its simple form; sometimes also it gives the idea of eminence. *Exam.* পরাক্রম, *power ;* পরাজয়, *conquest ;* পরামনন, *repentance ;* পরাবর্ত্তন, *a returning.*

অপ conveys the idea of privation or ablation. *Exam.* অপযশ, *dishonour ;* অপমান, *disgrace.*

সং gives the idea of society, amelioration, or augmentation. *Exam.* সম্মিলিত, *mixed with ;* সম্পুর্ণ, *complete.*

নি expresses the idea of completeness, excellence, or certainty. *Exam.* নিবিড়, *thick as a forest.* নিবারণ, *complete prohibition.*

অব gives the idea of ablation or privation. *Exam.* অবকৃষ্ট, *bad, deteriorated.*

অনু denotes following, consequent upon, or according to. *Exam.* অনুকারী, *imitating ;* অনুসন্ধান, *search, intention ;* অনুতাপ, *repentance.*

নির্ expresses privation, negation, and sometimes amelioration. *Exam.* নিরাকার, *without form ;* নিস্তার, *deliverance, salvation.*

দুর্ expresses deterioration or difficulty in the performing of the action. *Exam.* দুরাচার, *wicked ;* দুর্ম্মতি, *wicked ;* দুষ্কর, *difficult to be done ;* দুর্লভ, *difficultly attainable ;* দুর্গম, *scarcely passable.*

বি gives the idea of augmentation or privation. *Exam.* বিমোচন, *complete liberation ;* বিলম্ব, *delay.*

অধি gives the idea of possession. *Exam.* অধিকরণ, *a placing in ;* অধিষ্ঠাতা, *one who presides over.*

সু expresses excellence, abundance, and ease in performing the action. সুমতি, *well-disposed ;* সুবাণী, *good words ;* সুলভ, *easily obtainable.*

উৎ gives the idea of elevation. *Exam.* উদ্যোগ, *industry, stimulation.*

পরি indicates completeness, or the universal application

of the action. *Exam.* পরিপূর্ণ, *quite full, complete.* পরিজন, *attendants.*

প্রতি gives the idea of remuneration, or reciprocity. *Exam.* প্রত্যুত্তর, *a reply.* প্রত্যুপকার, *a grateful return.*

অভি gives the idea of direction towards an object. *Exam.* অভিমুখ, *facing, looking towards.* অভিমান, *pride, self-esteem.*

অতি gives the idea of augmentation or excess. *Exam.* অত্যন্ত, *exceedingly,* অতিশয়, *excessive.*

অপি gives the idea of augmentation, or certainty. *Exam.* অপিধান, *disappearing, concealment.*

উপ gives the idea of vicinity, or resemblance. *Exam.* কথা, *a word;* উপকথা, *title, tattle.* পথ, *a road;* উপপথ, *a by-way.* দ্বীপ, *a continent;* উপদ্বীপ, *an island.*

আ conveys the idea of extension. *Exam.* আক্রোশ, *displeasure;* আসমুদ্র, *to the sea.*

Examples to illustrate the powers of the inseparable Prepositions.

The root কৃ in its various forms becomes করণ, *a doing;* ক্রিয়া, *an action;* কৃত, *done;* কৃতি, *an action;* কারক, *a cause;* and several other words which, compounded with the prepositions, form new words. *Exam.* অনুকরণ, *an imitation;* দুষ্ক্রিয়া, *wickedness;* প্রকৃত, *properly done;* সংস্কৃত, *compact, consecrated;* বিকৃতি, *transformation, transmutation;* অধিকার, *a possession;* সুক্রিয়া, *a good action;* পরিষ্কার, *cleanness, purity;* প্রতিকার, *the returning of an action, a remedy;* উপকার, *assistance;* আকার, *a form;* নিরাকার, *without form;* and ব্যাকরণ, *a grammar.*

মান, *honour, measure,* is compounded with several prepositions; and almost every word in the language admits them. *Exam.* প্রমাণ, *a proof;* অপমান, *dishonour;* সম্মান, *honour;* অনুমান, *a guess, an inference;* নির্ম্মাণ, *a making, creating;* বিমান, *a chariot;* পরিমাণ, *a measure;* অভিমান, *self-honour, tenaciousness of honour;* উন্মান, *a weighing,* &c.

CONJUNCTIONS.

10. Conjunctions admit of no inflection. The following are the most common:

এবং, *and;* বরং, *rather;* ও, *and, also, moreover.*
কিন্তু, *but;* কেননা, যেহেতুক, *for, because.*
কি, কিম্বা, কিবা, *or.*
তবে, *then.*
বা, *or, and.*
অতএব, *therefore.*
এতদর্থে, *wherefore.*
একারণে, এজন্যে, এনিমিত্তে, *because.*
তবু, তমু, *notwithstanding, then.*
যদি, যদ্যপি, যদ্যপিস্যাৎ, *if.*
তথাপি, *yet, then, certainly.*
কদাচিৎ, *perhaps, at any time.*
নতু, নতুবা, *otherwise.*
অপর, *moreover, so, also.*
অপি, *also,* is affixed to words, as যদ্যপি, *if also.*
অনন্তর, *likewise, afterwards.*

INTERJECTIONS.

11. These are but few. The following are most commonly used:

Expressions of Distress.

বাপরে২, *O father! father!*
ত্রাহি২, *save! save!*
হায়২, *Oh!*

Of Pain.

ইঃ, উঃ, *Oh!*

Of Surprise.

বাহবাহ্, *surprising!*

Of Pity.

আহা, *Oh what distress!*
উহুঃ, *what shall I do!*

Rules to direct in the pronunciation of the INHERENT VOWEL *at the end of a word.*

1. This mark ্ (though often omitted) should always be inserted when a consonant has no inherent vowel.

2. The final অ is omitted in the pronunciation of substantives which have only two letters. *Exam.* মন, *mind;* জল, *water;* জপ, *religious repetition;* বাঁশ, *a bamboo;* খাদ, *a pit;* ক্ষীর, *milk.*

3. In numerals, and in the interrogative কোন্, the

vowel is not sounded with the last letter, but it must be sounded in কোন, *any*. *Exam.* এক, *one* ; পাঁচ, *five.*

4. The র্ of the possessive case never admits the pronunciation of the vowel after it. *Exam.* তাহার্, *his.*

5. In the first person of the second aorist, and the imperfect and pluperfect tenses of verbs of the indicative mode, and in the subjunctive preter, the final ম্ has no inherent vowel. *Exam.* করিতাম্, *I used to do* ; করিলাম্, *I did;* করিয়াছিলাম্, *I had done* ; যদি আমি করিতাম্, *If I had done.*

6. The final ন্ of the third person honorific, the final letter of the second and third persons of the imperative inferior, and the third person of the imperative honorific, do not admit the pronunciation of the vowel after them. *Exam.* করিলেন্, *he did;* করিবেন্, *he will do* ; কর্, *do* ; করুক, *let him do* ; করুন্, *let him do.*

7. Passive participles of two letters, ending in ন or ত, and all the enclitic particles, must have the last vowel expressed. *Exam.* কৃত, *done* ; হত, *smitten.*

8. The vowel must be constantly pronounced after a compound letter. *Exam.* কৃষ্ণ, *black*, also *the name of a Hindoo god* ; বংশ, *a family* ; দীর্ঘ, *long* ; মুক্ত, *liberated.*

SECTION X.

OF THE JUNCTION OF LETTERS, (সন্ধি.)

The permutation of letters when two words or syllables are so brought into contact that the final of the one coalesces with the initial of the other, is called S*u*ndh*i*, or joining. This permutation takes place in the final of the first member, or the initial of the last, or in both. This junction of words is not always necessary, yet, being in general use, and sometimes indispensable, the rules by which it is affected are introduced here.

To simplify the rules for this permutation of letters, the alphabet is thrown into an artificial form, as follows:

অ ই উ ঋ ঌ ক   এ ও ঙ ঐ ঔ চ
হ য ব র ল   ঞ ণ ন ঙ ম
ঝ ঢ ধ ঘ ভ   জ ড় দ গ ব
খ ফ ছ ঠ থ   চ ট ত ক প
শ ষ স.

Any two letters in this scheme, including all the intermediate ones, are called সমাহার or প্রত্যাহার, viz. *a collection.*

N. B. The ক, ঙ, and চ of the first line are put for the sake of pronouncing the S*u*mahar*us*, but must not be reckoned among the letters.

When any two of these letters are mentioned, the intermediate ones are included. *Exam.* অ—চ্ is all the vowels; ই—চ্ all the vowels except অ and আ (the long vowels being included in their similar short ones); ই—ক্ is ই, উ, ঋ, ঌ; য্—ণ is all the semi-vowels, and ঞ—ম্ all the nasals. Thus also of any other.

The change of ই to এ,
উ—ও,
ঋ—অর,
and ঌ to অল, is called goon.

The change of অ to আ;	ঌ to আল,
ই—ঐ,	এ — ঐ,
উ—ঔ,	and ও to ঔ,
ঋ—আর,	is called vriddhi.

S*u*ndh*i* is divided into two parts, viz. the junction of vowels, and that of consonants.

The Junction of Vowels.

1. When two similar vowels come together, they coalesce, and form one long vowel. *Exam.* মশা, *a musquito,* and অরি, *an enemy,* form মশারি, *musquito curtains.*

2. ই—ক্, viz. ই, উ, ঋ, and ঌ, (including their similar long vowels) if they follow অ or আ, coalesce therewith, making the change called goon; but এ—চ্, viz. এ, ঐ, ও or ঔ, following অ or আ, require the change called vriddhi. *Exam.* পরম, *good,* and ঈশ্বর, *God,* form পরমেশ্বর; তব, *thy,* and ওষ্ঠ, *a lip,* form তবৌষ্ঠ.

3. If ঋত, *affected with,* follow অ or আ, to form a compound adjective, the collision is made by vr*i*ddh*i*. This is also the case with the word ঋণ, *a loan,* when it

follows a few other words. *Exam.* তৃষ, and ঋত, form তৃষার্ত্ত, *thirst ;* দশ, *ten,* and ঋণ, *a loan,* form, দশার্ণ, *a loan of ten (rupees).*

N. B. If a preposition ending in অ or আ precede a verb with an initial এ or ও, the change is made by goon instead of vriddh*i*.

4. If a final vowel, অ and আ excepted, be followed by an initial dissimilar vowel, the following change is required in forming the junction :

ই	and ঈ	become	য.
উ	and ঊ	....	ব.
ঋ	and ৠ	....	র.
ঌ	and ৡ	....	ল.
এ		becomes	অয়্.
ও		....	অব্
ঐ		....	আয়্, and
ঔ		....	আব্.

Exam. ইতি, *this,* and আদি, *first,* form ইত্যাদি ; নববধূ, *a new wife,* and আগমন, *a coming,* form নববধ্বাগমন.

Of the Permutation of Consonants.

5. If a letter of the fourth class (ত—বর্গ) precede one of the second (চ—বর্গ), or of the third (ট—বর্গ), it is changed into that letter. *Exam.* তৎ, *that,* and চেষ্টা, *search,* form তচ্চেষ্টা, *that search.* সৎ, *good,* and জাত, *born,* form সজ্জাত, *born of a good (family).*

6. A letter of the fourth class, followed by শ, is changed to its corresponding letter in the second class. *Exam.* তৎ, that, শরীর, *the body,* form তচ্ছরীর, *that body.*

7. স followed by শ, or any other letter of the second class, becomes শ; followed by a letter of the third class it becomes ষ. *Exam.* মনস, *the mind,* and চারু, *excellent,* form মনশ্চারু, *a good mind;* ধনুস, *a bow,* and টঙ্কার, *the twang of the bow-string,* form ধনুষ্টঙ্কার, *the twang of the bow.*

8. Any letter of the fourth class preceded by ষ, is changed to its corresponding letter in the third class. *Exam.* ষষ্ঠ, *the sixth,* formed from ষষ্ and থ.

9. If the first, second, or fourth letter of any class be followed by the third or fourth of that or any other class, it will be changed into the third letter of its own class. ঋক্ and বেদ, become ঋগ্বেদ, *the* Rik-*Veda.*

10. Any letter of the fourth class preceding ল is changed to ল. *Exam.* সৎ, *good,* and লোক, *a person,* form সল্লোক, *a good man.*

11. The first letter of any class, if followed by a vowel, a semi-vowel, a nasal, or the third or fourth letter of any class, will be changed into the third letter of its own class. *Exam.* তৎ, *that,* and উপর, *above,* form তদুপর, *upon that;* সৎ, *good,* and গুণ, *a quality,* form সদ্গুণ, *a good quality.*

12. If শ followed by a vowel, a semi-vowel or a nasal follow the first letter of any class, it becomes ছ. হ in the same circumstances is changed to the fourth letter in that class. *Exam.* অপ্, *water,* and শয়ন, *lying down,* form অপ্ছয়ন, *lying in water,* বাক্, *a word,* and হনন, *a smiting,* form বাগ্ঘনন, *a smiting by words.*

13. The first letter of any class followed by a nasal is changed into the nasal of its own class. *Exam.* তৎ, *that,* and মধ্য, *in the midst,* form তন্মধ্য, *in the midst of that.*

14. A nasal, preceding a letter of any class besides its own, is changed to the nasal of that class to form the junction. If followed by a miscellaneous letter, it becomes ঙ or ং. *Exam.* শম্, *welfare,* and কর, *a doer,* form শঙ্কর, *a promoter of good.*

15. A final ঙ, ণ, ন, or ছ, preceded by a short vowel, is doubled if followed by a vowel. *Exam.* সন্, *pure,* and আত্মা, *a spirit,* form সন্নাত্মা, *a pure spirit,* বৃক্ষ, *a tree,* and ছায়া, *shade,* form বৃক্ষচ্ছায়া, *the shadow of a tree.*

16. ঃ becomes স, when followed by any letter, except a compound one, of which the first member is চ, ছ, ট, ঠ, ত or থ, and the last শ, ষ or স. *Exam.* the preposition দুঃ, (দুর,) followed by প্রাপ্য, *attainable,* form দুষ্প্রাপ্য, *difficult to be obtained.*

17. ঃ following any vowel except অ and আ, becomes র if followed by a vowel, a semi-vowel, a nasal, or the third or fourth letter of any class. *Exam.* হবিঃ, *ghee,* and ভোক্তা, *an eater,* form হবির্ভোক্তা, *a ghee-eater.*

18. ঃ following অ is changed to উ, if followed by অ, a semi-vowel, a nasal, or the third or fourth letter of any class. *Exam.* ততঃ, *than that,* and অধিক, *more,* form ততোধিক, *more than that.*

19. ঃ following অ or আ is rejected, if followed by a vowel, a semi-vowel, a nasal, or the third or fourth letter of any class. *Exam.* অতঃ and এব form অতএব, *therefore.*

It may be remarked here, that when ন follows র, ঋ, ৠ, or ষ, in the same word, or in the same member of a compound word, it must be changed to ণ, except it be final.

This change is not prevented if any letter of the first or fifth class, a vowel, a semi-vowel, or ং intervene, (ব্যব-ধান.)

N. B. The ং here meant is only that which is produced from ন্ or ম্.

When স follows any letter of the first class, any vowel, অ excepted, or a semi-vowel, it must always be changed to ষ, unless it be at the end of a word. This is not prevented if ং intervene.

SECTION XI.

Of Syntax.

1. A word or sentence which expresses or describes any quality of a noun or verb is called বিশেষণ, (*v*ishesh*u*-*n*a,) and the word, the quality of which is expressed, is called বিশেষ্য, (*v*ish*i*shy*a*.)

2. If the *v*ish*i*shy*a* be a noun or pronoun, the *v*ishe-sh*una* is its adjective ; if a verb, its adverb.

3. Sometimes the *v*ishesh*una* consists of a sentence or sentences made up of subordinate *v*ishesh*una*s and vish*i*-shy*as*. *Exam.* অভিষেকার্থ সিংহাসনসমীপোপস্থিত শ্রীভোজ-রাজকে দেখিয়া পঞ্চদশী পুত্তলিকা কহিলেন, *the fifteenth image, seeing king* Bhoja, *(who was) near the throne for the purpose of anointment, said.* In this sentence অভিষেকার্থ-সিংহাসনসমীপোপস্থিত, *for the purpose of anointment situated near the throne,* is the *v*isheshun*a* of শ্রীভোজরাজকে, the *v*ish*i*shy*a*.

4. A *v*isheshuna must be of the same gender with its *v*ish*i*shy*a*. যুবা পুরুষ, *a young man,* যুবতী স্ত্রী, *a young woman.*

5. The *v*isheshu*na* usually precedes the *v*ish*i*shy*a*. *Exam.* মদনসঞ্জীবন ইহা শুনিয়া তথাতে গিয়া প্রত্যক্ষতো দেখিয়া শ্রীবিক্রমাদিত্যের দগ্ধ শরীরে অমৃতাভিষেক দ্বারা পুর্ব্ববৎ নির্ব্রণনির্ব্যথশরীর করিল, Mudunusunjeev*una hearing this, having gone* THITHER, *and having seen the evidence,*

by anointing VIKRUMADITYU'S BURNT *body with* umrita, *made him* SCARLESS *and* PAINLESS-BODIED AS BEFORE.

6. In forming sentences, the agent is usually placed first, the object second, and the verb last. *Exam.* মন্ত্রী রাজাকে কহিলেন, *the counsellor said to the king.*

7. If a long sentence, or several sentences describe the object of a verb, they are introduced first; after which the thing described by the sentence is put in the accusative case, and followed by the agent, which immediately precedes the verb. *Exam.* যে জন অতিশয় দুরাচার এবং কাহারু কথা শুনে না এবং সর্ব্বদা ক্রুদ্ধ তাহাকে তুমি কিছু কহিও না, *say nothing to that man who is wicked, and minds not what any one says, and is always angry.*

8. A verb agrees with its agent, or nominative case, in person, number, and quality. *Exam.* আমি করিতেছি, *I am doing;* আমরা বলিয়াছি, *we have spoken;* তুই গিয়াছিস্, *thou wentest;* তিনি যাইবেন্, *he will go.**

N. B. The adjective and pronoun being generally compounded with the substantive, are to be accounted but as one word. In this case the concord is disregarded.

9. Active verbs, those of motion, giving, and speaking excepted, govern their object in the accusative case. *Exam.* তিনি কর্ম্ম করিলেন, *he did the business;* আমি তাহাকে দুর করিলাম, *I removed him.*

10. The verb করণ, *to do;* হওন, *to be,* and a few others,

* The agent of verbs is often omitted, being included in the verb itself. The singular and plural of Bengalee verbs being the same, many of the rules of concord, so necessary in other languages, are useless in this.

are constructed with substantives, adjectives, or passive participles. *Exam.* সে নাশ করে, *he works destruction* or *destroys ;* সে নষ্ট করে, *he makes destroyed,* viz. *destroys ;* সে নষ্ট হইয়াছে, *it is destroyed.*

11. When substantives are constructed with করণ, they govern a word either in the accusative or possessive case; when with হওন, only in the possessive. When adjectives or passive participles are constructed with করণ, they always govern a word in the accusative case ; when with হওন, they govern a nominative. *Exam.* সে তাহাকে সম্মান করিল or তাহার সম্মান করিল, *he honoured him ;* তাহার সম্মান হইয়াছে, *his honour is (obtained) ;* আমি তাহাকে নষ্ট করিব, *I will destroy him,* (viz. *make him destroyed ;*) তিনি নষ্ট হইয়াছেন, *he is ruined.*

12. Sometimes the gerund of a verb is the agent of another verb. *Exam.* বড় আনন্দ করিতে হবে, *great rejoicings must be made ;* literally, *to make great rejoicing will be.*

13. The instrumental cause of any action must be expressed in the third case. *Exam.* তিনি আপন বলেতে জয় করিলেন, *he conquered by his own strength.*

14. The agent of a passive verb must be in the third case. The passive voice is sometimes expressed by the active form. *Exam.* অনেক লোক বাঘে খাইয়াছে, *many people were eaten by tigers.* জগৎ ঈশ্বরেতে সৃষ্ট ছিল, *the world was created by God.* অনেক যত্নেতে সে ক্রিয়া করা গেল, *that business was done with great labour.*

15. Verbs which express the performance of an action

by means of an instrument, sometimes govern the participles দিয়া, করিয়া, &c. instead of the instrumental case, *Exam.* আমি ছুরীতে কাটিলাম, or ছুরী দিয়া কাটিলাম, *I cut it with a knife.*

16. Verbs of giving, of doing obeisance, of speaking, advising, &c. govern either a dative or an accusative. *Exam.* আমি বন্ধুরে or বন্ধুকে দি, নমস্কার করি, কহি, or পরামর্শ দি, *I give, salute, speak,* or *give advice to my friend.*

17. লওন, পাওন, and all verbs which signify going from, falling from, gaining from, or obtaining from, a person or thing, govern an ablative case. *Exam.* তিনি আপন পিতার নিকটহইতে গেলেন, *he went from his father.* বালক বৃক্ষহইতে পড়িল, *the child fell from the tree.*

18. The comparative particle *than* is generally expressed by the ablative in হইতে. *Exam.* এ জল সে জলহইতে নির্ম্মল আছে, *this water is cleaner than that.*

19. Verbs of motion to or towards a place, govern either the accusative or locative case, but generally the former; those of entering, living, acting, or remaining in a place, always govern a locative case. *Exam.* সে শ্রীরামপুর গিয়াছে, *he is gone to Serampore,* or আমি গ্রামে যাই, *I go to the village;* সিন্দুকে আছে, *it is in the chest;* তাহা ঘরে থোও, *put it in the house.*

20. The preterperfect tense of the verb হওন, *to be,* is used instead of the present, when we speak of any thing as completed, or then present. *Exam.* এমন কথা হইয়াছে, *there is such talk,* or *such a report.*

21. The syllables কো and তো are frequently added to the negative preter. *Exam.* আমিতো করিনি, *I have not done it ;* আমি বলিনি কো, *I have not said it.*

22. Comparative sentences, constructed with a relative and antecedent pronoun, or with adverbs answering to each other, are generally made in the form of an antithesis, the relative member preceding the antecedent. The pronouns in such sentences should precede the noun as its *visheshuna*, and are seldom permitted to follow it as introducing an explanatory word or sentence. *Exam.* যে মনুষ্যের বিদ্যা না হইল সে পশু কেন নয়? *why is not that man a beast who has no wisdom?* Literally, *what man's wisdom, is not, that (man) why not a beast?* তোমায় যদি এ সকল গুণ থাকে তবে এ সিংহাসনে বসিবার যোগ্য হও, *if you have all these virtues, you are fit to sit on this throne.*

23. In negative sentences the particle নয় is used when any property or quality is denied concerning any person or thing. *Exam.* সে গরু নয়, *that is not a cow.*

24. When the verb is supposed, the negative particle is inflected, and supplies its place. *Exam.* আমার কিছু টাকা নয়, *I have no money ;* literally, *my any money is not.*

25. When an inferior addresses a superior he is said *to petition* or *represent to him* (নিবেদন), and the superior is said *to command* (আজ্ঞা), though there be nothing of request or injunction in what is said. *Exam.* ভৃত্যেরা এই সকল শাস্ত্রোক্ত রাজাভিষেক সামগ্রী আয়োজন করিয়া রাজার নিকটে নিবেদন করিল, *the servants, having collected all those shastra-commanded king-anointing materials, told the king.*

আপনি যে আজ্ঞা করিয়াছেন সে প্রমাণ বটে, *what your honour has said is true.*

26. Whenever an inferior speaks about a superior, the honorific style must be used. It is sometimes used when a superior speaks of an inferior. The pronoun তুই is seldom used except to denote familiarity or contempt. মুই is used when any one speaks with humility, or intends to abase himself in addressing a superior. এ, ও, সে and যে neither express honour nor contempt. *Exam.* তিনি সে কথা কহিলেন, *he said that.* তুই কি বলিস্, *what dost thou gabble about?* মুই মহাশয়ের নিকট নিবেদন করি, *I request your honour.*

27. An affirmation is frequently made by asking a question. *Exam.* এত ঔষধ কি খাইতে পারি? *can I take so much medicine?* meaning *I cannot take so much.* আমি কি তাহা করিব না? *will I not do it?* viz. *I will certainly do it.*

28. The necessity of an action is frequently denoted by আবশ্যক or প্রয়োজন, *necessity,* governing the neuter verb, as তোমার নদী পার করার আবশ্যক আছে, *you must cross the river.* সে কার্য্য করণেতে কি প্রয়োজন, *what necessity is there to do that?*

29. An interrogative sentence is usually formed by inserting কি before the verb, but as near it as possible. *Exam.* তুমি কি জান না? *do you not know?* তুমি কি সে কথা শুন নাই? *have you not heard that account?*

Of Numerals.

Cardinal.	Numerical figure.	Ordinal.
এক, *one.*	১	প্রথম, *first.*
দুই, *two.*	২	দ্বিতীয়, *second.*
তিন, *three.*	৩	তৃতীয়, *third.*
চারি, *four.*	৪	চতুর্থ, *fourth.*
পাঁচ, *five.*	৫	পঞ্চম, *fifth.*
ছয়, *six.*	৬	ষষ্ঠ, *sixth.*
সাত, *seven.*	৭	সপ্তম, *seventh.*
আট, *eight.*	৮	অষ্টম, *eighth.*
নয়, *nine.*	৯	নবম, *ninth.*
দশ, *ten.*	১০	দশম, *tenth.*

এগার or একাদশ, *eleven.*
বারো or দ্বাদশ, *twelve.*
তেরো or ত্রয়োদশ, *thirteen.*
চৌদ্দ or চতুর্দ্দশ, *fourteen.*
পনেরো or পঞ্চদশ, *fifteen.*
ষোল or ষোড়শ, *sixteen.*
সতের or সপ্তদশ, *seventeen.*
আটার or অষ্টাদশ, *eighteen.*
ঊনিশ or ঊনবিংশতি, *nineteen.*
বিশ or বিংশতি, *twenty*; কুড়ি, *a score.*
একুশ, *twenty-one.*
বাইস, *twenty-two.*
তেইশ, *twenty-three.*
চব্বিশ, *twenty-four.*
পঁচিশ, *twenty-five.*
ছাব্বিশ, *twenty-six.*
সাতাইশ, *twenty-seven.*
আটাইশ, *twenty-eight.*
ঊনত্রিশ, *twenty-nine.*
ত্রিশ or ত্রিংশৎ, *thirty.*
একত্রিশ, *thirty-one.*
বত্রিশ, *thirty-two.*
তেত্রিশ, *thirty-three.*
চৌত্রিশ, *thirty-four.*
পঁয়ত্রিশ, *thirty-five.*
ছত্রিশ, *thirty-six.*
সাঁইত্রিশ, *thirty-seven.*
আটত্রিশ, *thirty-eight.*
ঊনচল্লিশ, *thirty-nine.*
চল্লিশ or চত্বারিংশৎ, *forty.*
একচল্লিশ, *forty-one.*
বিয়াল্লিশ, *forty-two.*
তেতাল্লিশ, *forty-three.*

চৌয়াল্লিশ, *forty-four.*
পঁয়তাল্লিশ, *forty-five.*
ছচল্লিশ, *forty-six.*
সাতচল্লিশ, *forty-seven.*
আটচল্লিশ, *forty-eight.*
ঊনপঞ্চাশ, *forty-nine.*
পঞ্চাশ, *fifty.*
একান্ন, *fifty-one.*
বায়ান্ন, *fifty-two.*
তিপ্পান্ন, *fifty-three.*
চৌয়ান্ন, *fifty-four.*
পঞ্চান্ন, *fifty-five.*
ছাপ্পান্ন, *fifty-six.*
সাতান্ন, *fifty-seven.*
আটান্ন, *fifty-eight.*
ঊনষাইট, *fifty-nine.*
ষাইট or ষষ্টি, *sixty.*
একষট্টি, *sixty-one.*
বাষট্টি, *sixty-two.*
তেষট্টি, *sixty-three.*
চৌষট্টি, *sixty-four.*
পঁয়ষট্টি, *sixty-five.*
ছেষট্টি, *sixty-six.*
সাতষট্টি, *sixty-seven.*
আটষট্টি, *sixty-eight.*
ঊনসত্যর, *sixty-nine.*
সত্যর or সপ্ততি, *seventy.*
একাত্তর, *seventy-one.*
বাহাত্তর, *seventy-two.*
তেহাত্তর, *seventy-three.*
চৌহাত্তর, *seventy-four.*
পঁচাত্তর, *seventy-five.*
ছেহাত্তর, *seventy-six.*
সাতাত্তর, *seventy-seven.*
আটাত্তর, *seventy-eight.*
ঊনাশী, *seventy-nine.*
আশী or অশীতি, *eighty.*
একাশী, *eighty-one.*
বিরাশী, *eighty-two.*
তিরাশী, *eighty-three.*
চৌরাশী, *eighty-four.*
পঞ্চাশী, *eighty-five.*
ছেয়াশী, *eighty-six.*
সাতাশী or সপ্তাশী, *eighty-seven.*
অষ্টাশী, *eighty-eight.*
ঊননব্বই, *eighty-nine.*
নব্বই or নবতি, *ninety.*
একানব্বই, *ninety-one.*
বিরানব্বই, *ninety-two.*
তিরানব্বই, *ninety-three.*
চৌরানব্বই, *ninety-four.*
পঞ্চানব্বই, *ninety-five.*
ছেয়ানব্বই, *ninety-six.*
সাতানব্বই, *ninety-seven.*
আটানব্বই, *ninety-eight.*
নিরানব্বই, *ninety-nine,*
শত, *a hundred.*

1. Other numerals, from twenty upwards, are formed by prefixing এক, দ্বা, ত্রয়ো, চতুর, পঞ্চ, ষষ্ঠ, সপ্ত, and অষ্ট, to the even tens, viz. বিংশতি, ত্রিংশৎ, চত্বারিংশৎ, পঞ্চা-

শৎ, ষষ্টি, সপ্ততি, অশীতি, and নবতি. *Exam.* একবিংশতি, *twenty-one,* দ্বাবিংশতি, *twenty-two,* &c.

2. The numerals which express one less than even tens are formed by prefixing ঊন to the next even ten. *Exam.* ঊনত্রিংশৎ, *twenty-nine.* নিরানব্বই, *ninety-nine,* is an exception.

3. Ordinals are formed by affixing ত্রি or ই, to the first column of numerals. Those of the second column, or S*u*ngskrit*a* numerals, are given as far as ten. From ten to twenty they are the same as the cardinal numbers. The ordinals of even tens are made by affixing তম, or by omitting the last letter. From sixty upwards they are made by তম only. The intermediate ordinals are like the cardinal numbers. *Exam.* দশত্রি or দশই, *the tenth,* বিংশ or বিংশতিতম, *the twentieth.*

4. Multipliers are made by affixing গুণ to the cardinal number. *Exam.* তিনগুণ, *thrice,* পাঁচগুণ, *five times.*

5. Numeral adverbs, indicating a thing to be done at so many times, are formed by affixing দা to the cardinal number. *Exam.* একদা, *at once,* চতুর্দা, *at four times,* বহুদা, *many times,* সর্ব্বদা, *always.*

6. Repetitive numbers are made by affixing বার to the cardinal. *Exam.* আমি তিনবার কহিলাম, *I spake three times.*

7. Numerals agreeing with the English ones ending in -fold are made by affixing ধা to cardinals. *Exam.* দ্বিধা, *two-fold,* চতুর্ধা, *four-fold,* বহুধা, *manifold.*

পোয়া, *a quarter,* অৰ্দ্ধ or অৰ্দ্ধেক, *half,* দেড়, *one and a half,* and আড়াই, *two and a half,* are irregular.

8. A quarter more than any even number, is expressed by affixing শওয়া to the number; an half more than an even number, by সাড়ে, and a quarter less than a given number by prefixing পৌনে. *Exam.* সওয়াতিন, *three and a quarter.* সাড়ে তিন, *three and a half.* পৌনে চারি, *three and three quarters,* or *a quarter less than four.*

9. Fractions are generally expressed by $\frac{1}{16}$ parts or anas, (an ana being the sixteenth part of a rupee.) *Exam.* সাত-আনা, *seven sixteenths ;* দশআনা, *ten sixteenths.*

Of Money, Weights and Measures.

There are two sorts of accounts kept in Bengal, viz. পাকা and কাঁচা, which are known by তঙ্কা being written over the পাকা account, and কড়ি over the কাঁচা. The figures for the cowries, &c. are the same in both ; but in the পাকা account টাকা or rupee, is the highest denomination, and in the কাঁচা account the কাহন.

Money.

4 cowries (কড়ি, marked thus, ꠷) make 1 gunda (গণ্ডা, marked ১). N. B. When a numeral is prefixed, the cowry is called কড়া, kura. *Exam.* এক কড়া, দুই কড়া, &c.

20 cowries, or 5 gundas, 1 boori (বুড়ি, or damri, দামড়ি ৫).

20 gundas ... 1 pun (পণ /).

4 puns ...... 1 ana, chouk, or dam, (আনা, চৌক, দাম).

16 puns ...... 1 kahun (কাহন ১).

16 anas ...... 1 rupee (টাকা ১).

Whatever the rupee be valued at in the bazar, the fourth part is called a sicca (সিকা ।০).

All articles bought and sold by the tale, are counted by gundas and puns.

Weights.

8 *rutis** (রত্তি, or seeds of abrus precatorious, called কুঁচ) ... ... make 1 masa (মাষা).
10 masa ... ... „ 1 tola (তোলা).
4 tolas ... ... „ 1 chutack (ছটাক).
4 chutacks ... ... „ 1 poa, or quarter (পোয়া).
4 poas, or 16 chutacks „ 1 ser (সের).
40 sers, ... „ 1 mun (মোন).

Long Measure.

3 Barley corns (যব) ... 1 ungooli, or *breadth of the finger*, (অঙ্গুলি.)
4 ungoolis ... ... 1 moot, or *hand's-breadth*, (মুট.)
3 moots ... ... 1 bighut, or *span*, (বিঘত.)
2 spans ... ... 1 hata, or *cubit*, (হাত.)
4 hatas ... ... 1 dhunoo, or *fathom*, (ধনু.)
1000 dhunoos ... ... 1 kros, or koos, (ক্রোশ.)
4 kros ... ... 1 yojun, (যোজন.)

Dry Measure.

4 reks (রেক), or palees (পালি), 1 don (দোন), or dron (দ্রোণ) or pussuri (পসরি), equal to 5 sers.
4 drons ... ... 1 arhi (আড়ি).
20 drons, or 5 arhis, ... 1 suli (সলি).
4 sulis ... ... 1 bish (বিষ).
16 bish ... ... 1 pouti (পৌটি).

* According to the rules observed by physicians, 10 *rutis* are a masa, and 8 masa a tola.

Time.

The time while one can deliberately pronounce ten long syllables is ... ... 1 pran.

6 prans	1 p*u*l.
60 puls	1 d*u*nd*a*.
60 dundas	1 day.
7 days	1 week.

The days of the week.

The days of the week are named from the Planets.

রবিবার, Sunday,	from রবি, the sun.
সোমবার, Monday,	„ সোম, the moon.
মঙ্গলবার, Tuesday,	„ মঙ্গল, Mars.
বুধবার, Wednesday,	„ বুধ, Mercury.
বৃহস্পতিবার, Thursday,	„ বৃহস্পতি, Jupiter.
শুক্রবার, Friday,	„ শুক্র, Venus.
শনিবার, Saturday,	„ শনি, Saturn.

A day is divided into two parts দিনমান, viz. the time from sun-rising to sun-setting, and রাত্রিমান, the time from sun-setting to sun-rising. Each of these is subdivided into four equal parts, called প্রহর, or watches, one of which is nearly equal to three English hours, but varying with the season.

Of the Hindoo Months.

The Hindoo months always begin at what they call the সংক্রান্তি, viz. the moment of the sun's entering any sign of the Zodiac.

বৈশাখ, the latter part of	April, and former part of	May.
জ্যৈষ্ঠ,	May,	June.
আষাঢ়,	June,	July.
শ্রাবণ,	July,	August.
ভাদ্র,	August,	September.
আশ্বিন,	September,	October.
কার্ত্তিক,	October,	November.
অগ্রহায়ণ,	November,	December.
পৌষ,	December,	January.
মাঘ,	January,	February.
ফাল্গুণ,	February,	March.
চৈত্র,	March,	April.

The month is divided into two পক্ষ, or sides (of the moon), the time from the change (অমাবস্যা) to the full moon (পূর্ণিমা) is called the শুক্লপক্ষ, *bright side*, from the full to the change কৃষ্ণপক্ষ, *the dark side.* A lunar day is called তিথি.

Contractions.

The following are often used in writing:

কিং for কিসমত, *a village* or *division.*
— কিস্তি, *a boat.*
— কিস্তিবন্দি, *a rent-roll, an agreement to pay by instalments.*

চাং — চালান, *an invoice.*
— চাকর, *a servant.*

জাং — জামিন, *a surety* or *security.*

জোং — জোড়', *a pair* (or *suit*) *of any thing.*

জিং — জিম্মা, *in trust*, or, *in the charge of.*
— জিনিস, *goods.*

নং — নগদ, *ready money.*

তাং — তালুক, *a talook* or *small jumeendaree.*
— তারিখ, *the date* or *day of the month.*

তং — তরফ, *a side*, or *towards.*

দং — দর, *price.*

— দরুণ, *on account of.*

পং — পরগনা, *a purguna* or *hundred.*

পাং — পাইক, *paik* or *footman.*

পেং — পেয়াদা, *a peada (a footman* or *messenger.)*

বাং — বাবদ, *on account of*, or *belonging to.*

মং -- মণ্ডল, *a mundul*, or *chief person in a village.*

মাং — মাহ, *the moon, a month.*

— মারফত, *by the hands of.*

— মহম্মদ, *Mahummud.*

মেং — *the English Mr.*

মোং — মোকাম, *a place, prefixed to the name of any place.*

লাং — লাগাইদ, *ending with.*

সাং — সাকিম, *an habitation.*

হাং — হাওলাত, *to the care of.*

ইং — ইস্তক, *beginning with.*

FINIS.